The Science of Interper

A Practical Guide to Building Healthy Relationships, Improving Your Soft Skills and Learning Effective Communication

Positive Psychology Coaching Series

Copyright © 2018 by Ian Tuhovsky

Author's blog: www.mindfulnessforsuccess.com
Author's Amazon profile: amazon.com/author/iantuhovsky
Instagram profile: https://instagram.com/mindfulnessforsuccess

All rights reserved. No part of this publication may be reproduced, stored in a retrieval system, or transmitted, in any form or by any means, electronic, mechanical, photocopying, recording or otherwise without the prior written permission of the author and the publishers.

The scanning, uploading, and distribution of this book via the Internet, or via any other means, without the permission of the author is illegal and punishable by law.
Please purchase only authorized electronic editions, and do not participate in or encourage electronic piracy of copyrighted materials.

Important
The book is not intended to provide medical advice or to take the place of medical advice and treatment from your personal physician. Readers are advised to consult their own doctors or other qualified health professionals regarding the treatment of medical conditions. The author shall not be held liable or responsible for any misunderstanding or misuse of the information contained in this book. The information is not indeed to diagnose, treat or cure any disease.
It's important to remember that the author of this book is not a doctor/therapist/medical professional. Only opinions based upon his own personal experiences or research are cited. The author does not offer medical advice or prescribe any treatments. For any health or medical issues – you should be talking to your doctor first.

Please be aware that every e-book and "short read" I publish is truly written by me, with thoroughly researched content 100% of the time. Unfortunately, there's a huge number of low quality, cheaply outsourced spam titles on Kindle non-fiction market these days, created by various Internet marketing companies. **I don't tolerate these books. I want to provide you with high quality, so** if you think that one of my books/short reads can be improved in some way, please contact me at: contact@mindfulnessforsuccess.com

I will be very happy to hear from you, because you are who I write my books for!

Introduction: Why You Need to Polish Your Relationship Skills 4

Part I – Laying The Groundwork For Healthy Relationships 10

Chapter 1: How Your Communication Skills Can Help You Choose the Right Partner 11

Chapter 2: Identifying & Handling Codependency 21

Chapter 3: Setting & Defending Boundaries In A Relationship 28

Chapter 4: Defining A Relationship 35

Chapter 5: Your Partner's Most Important Need, & How To Meet It 42

Chapter 6: How To Make Assertive Communication Work In Your Relationships ... 49

Chapter 7: How to Identify & Handle Verbal Abuse 57

Chapter 8: Dealing with Negative People 65

Chapter 9: Identifying & Handling Love Addiction 75

Part II – Developing the Communication Skills You Need For Great Relationships 83

Chapter 10: Understanding Different Communication Styles 84

Chapter 11: How to Validate Another Person (And Yourself!) 94

Chapter 12: How to Say "No" To Anyone 104

Chapter 13: How to Stop Having The Same Old Arguments 113

Chapter 14: Topics Couples Fight About Most Often 122

Chapter 15: How to Use Communication to Rebuild Trust & Prevent Jealousy 129

Chapter 16: Communication Tools That Will Rekindle the Flame In Romantic Relationships 135

Chapter 17: Effective Communication for Parents & Caregivers 138

Chapter 18: Communication Strategies for Friendships 144

Conclusion 150

My Free Gift to You – Get One of My Audiobooks for Free! 152

Recommended Reading for You 154

About The Author 169

Introduction: Why You Need to Polish Your Relationship Skills

By the end of high school, most of us have started to date, and most of us will have been in love at least once.[1] It's safe to say that romantic relationships are hugely important. It makes sense – after all, if we weren't interested in love and physical intimacy, our species wouldn't have lasted this long!

There's nothing quite like that feeling you get when you see someone who makes your heart race. When you fall in love, your brain releases a chemical called dopamine,[2] which triggers your neurological pleasure centers. It's no wonder that some people fall in love with love itself, and that romantic relationships play such a powerful role in our lives.

But if love is so natural, why aren't romantic relationships easy? We all know that they can get complicated quickly. Falling and staying in love is one of the biggest challenges we face.

For example, how many of us have happily dated someone for a few months, or even a couple of years, only to watch hopelessly as it fizzled out? This doesn't happen by chance.

There are good reasons why some couples make it and others don't last the distance. True, compatibility plays a big role. **However, the magic ingredient that makes for a wonderful relationship is good communication.** Once you understand how to really connect with another person and meet their needs, you can create deep, lasting intimacy.

As you might expect, psychologists and communication experts have spent a lot of time trying to pin down what it is that makes relationships so tough. It all boils down to a few key issues.

---

[1] Regan, P.C., Durvasula, R., Howell, L., Ureno, O., & Rea, M. (2004). Gender, Ethnicity, and the Developmental Timing of First Sexual and Romantic Experiences. *Social Behavior and Personality, 32, 7,* 667-676.
[2] Boyles, S. (2010). *Romantic Love Affects Your Brain Like a Drug.* Webmd.com

My argument is simple. If we all committed to improving our communication skills, we would all have much better love lives!

Here are the root causes of most relationship problems:

We have unrealistic expectations: Thanks to popular culture, lots of us grow up with a distorted view of romantic love. We are bombarded with movies, TV shows, and books that suggest love is easy. This means we might become dispirited when our relationships come up against even minor problems,[3] and we get depressed when they don't live up to our grand expectations.

Another common problem is that people assume a partner can fulfil all of their emotional needs, and they stop looking for happiness outside of that person. This can result in claustrophobic, unhealthy relationships.

The solution? We need to learn to communicate our wants, needs, and boundaries.

We assume that if you have to work at a relationship, it isn't worth having: There is still stigma attached to couples therapy, and people tend to assume that if two individuals are having trouble relating to one another, they should split up.

This attitude doesn't exactly encourage a positive approach to conflict. I'm willing to bet that a lot of broken relationships could have been salvaged, if only both partners had known how to communicate with one another.

The solution? We need to learn how to argue constructively, and how to resolve our differences.

We want to be right at all costs: If you would rather "win" an argument than reach a compromise, your relationship will suffer. If you focus on your own needs and opinions instead of taking the time to understand your partner's perspective, the two of you will drift apart.[4]

---

[3] Tartakovsky, M. (2016). *8 Surprising Myths About Relationships.*
[4] Other Live. (2017). *Tony Robbins: Why Relationships Are So Hard.* youtube.com

Those of us raised in cultures that place a lot of emphasis on "winning" an argument can find it really difficult to set aside our pride and put our partners first.

The solution? We need to approach relationships as collaborative projects, understand our partner's communication style, and be willing to make ourselves vulnerable by admitting when we are hurt.

We are in a time of social and cultural flux: I'm all for gender equality, and I think it's great that men and women can now experiment with different relationship arrangements.

For example, both men and women can ask each other out on dates, pursue careers, stay home to care for their children, and speak up for their rights. The downside? We've lost the traditional relationship templates that told us how relationships are "supposed" to work.

In days gone by, everyone knew what men and women were meant to do when dating (or "courting"). The man would initiate the dates, the woman would do most of the emotional labor that made the relationship run smoothly, and almost everyone got married before moving in together.

These days, it feels like anything and everything goes, which can make it hard for us to figure out what we actually want in a relationship. There's more analysis and problem-solving involved in dating these days, and it can all get pretty confusing.[5]

The solution? That's right – better communication! Being able to talk about our relationship preferences, and learning how to define our relationships, is the best way forward.

Those of you who have read my previous books will know that I'm passionate about communication skills. For years, I've been researching the secrets of the world's best communicators, and teaching my clients how to apply them in both their

---

[5] Karantzas, G. (n.d.) *This is why it's so hard to find love.* this.deakin.edu.au

professional and personal lives. So far, I have published two books on this fascinating topic: "Communication Skills Training" and "The Science of Effective Communication", both of which became Amazon Bestsellers and have been receiving very positive comments from my readers.

It's so rewarding when readers get in touch to let me know how much my books have helped them, and I'm always eager to learn from their feedback. When it became clear that my audience wanted help with their relationships, I knew what I had to do! I love passing on my knowledge, and so I was happy to write this guide to communication in interpersonal relationships.

In the first half of the book, you will develop the right relationship mindset that will set the stage for healthy, mature love. You'll learn how to navigate the early stages of dating, how to draw your boundaries, and how to handle the "Where is this relationship going?" talk with grace and dignity.

Even if you are already in a relationship, going back to basics and rethinking your approach to communication will result in a deeper bond between you and your partner.

I cringe when I look back over my relationship history. I dated several women during my late teens and early twenties, but I never seemed to get into a good, steady relationship.

Somehow, I'd always end up in petty fights with the girl I was dating, or I'd just feel as though something was missing between us. It wasn't until I started taking an interest in the psychology of human interaction that a lot of my dating disasters started to make sense.

As you read this book, you'll start to realize that you have the power to transform your love life for the better. How exciting is that? In the second half, you'll learn specific communication tactics that will get you through even the toughest parts of any romantic relationship.

You'll find out why you and your partner tend to fight about the same things over and over again, how to keep the spark alive in a long-term relationship, how to provide the validation that your partner craves, how to say "No" without damaging your bond, and much more. A lot of this advice is applicable to friendships and familial relationships too.

I know what you're thinking. "Communication skills" doesn't sound very romantic, does it? When I started researching this stuff, I found the science of relationships fascinating - but also a little depressing. I had to shed a lot of my illusions about love, dating, and marriage.

But guess what? Deliberately improving your relationship skills is a romantic thing to do, because it's the best path to true love. Learning how to engage with your partner, and actively working to make the relationship safe and happy, is one of the most loving acts of all.

Within a few weeks of reading up on the most common mistakes people make when trying to communicate with their dates, my love life started to improve. I noticed that the girl I was dating at the time suddenly started to make more time for me, and even began dropping hints that we might have a long-term future.

One particular incident proved that I was on the right track. We had decided to see a movie and grab coffee afterwards. She had picked the movie, and I hadn't realized until the opening minutes that it was an obscure arthouse title. To be honest, it was one of the most pointless, pretentious films I had ever seen.

After the film, my date asked me how I liked the movie. I opened my mouth to tell her precisely what I thought, but then something made me pause for a moment. I finally realized, at the age of 24, that this woman didn't actually want to hear my negative rant about subtitled French films.

What she truly needed was a validating, uplifting conversation, and an enriching exchange of views that would increase our intimacy and rapport.

Instead of launching into a tirade, I thanked her for the new experience, picked out a couple of things I managed to like about the film, and then asked her what she liked about it. I let her talk for ten minutes, and made sure that I validated her opinion the whole time. Only then did I offer any negative feedback. I kept my criticism brief, and emphasized that I respected her opinion.

Rather than focusing on the technical aspects of the film, I talked about how it had made me feel, and the old memories it had brought up for me. This encouraged her to open up about some personal events from her own past, and we grew closer as a result.

If I had not taken the time to learn about empathy and validation in relationships, that conversation would have ended on a sour note. She would have gone home after the date thinking that I was an insensitive jerk. As it was, we went on to date for another year before life circumstances forced us to break up.

It's worth noting that we are still friends today. Although she is now married, she has told me that I'm one of the most thoughtful, sensitive guys she ever dated. All I did was learn how to communicate with respect, empathize with her position, and share my opinion without triggering an argument. If I can do it, so can you!

I can't promise you a perfect partner or a perfect relationship. You should be suspicious of anyone who tells you that the perfect man or woman is out there, because they don't actually exist! But if you read and implement the advice in this book, I guarantee that your relationships will improve.

If you are single right now, this book still has a lot to offer you. Don't wait until you meet someone special. Brush up on your relationship skills now, and the next girl or guy you date will be blown away by your sensitivity, warmth, and fantastic personality. I can't promise that everyone will fall in love with you, but this book will definitely improve your chances of finding The One. I'm a romantic at heart, and believe that there really is someone out there for everyone. But nothing worth having ever came easy! It's time to take a close look at how you handle your relationships. Turn the page to get started.

Your Free Mindfulness E-book

I really appreciate the fact that you took an interest in my work!

I also think it's great you are into self-development and proactively making your life better.

Therefore, I would love to offer you a free, complimentary 120-page e-book.

It's about Mindfulness-Based Stress and Anxiety Management Techniques.

It will provide you with a solid foundation to kick-start your self-development success and help you become much more relaxed, while at the same time, becoming a more focused and effective person. All explained in plain English, it's a useful free supplement to this book.

To download your e-book, please visit:

http://www.tinyurl.com/mindfulnessgift

Enjoy!
Thanks again for being my reader! It means a lot to me!

Part I – Laying the Groundwork For Healthy Relationships

Chapter 1: How Your Communication Skills Can Help You Choose the Right Partner

Communication skills aren't just crucial in holding a relationship together. They make all the difference when it comes to choosing the right partner, building rapport, and moving your relationship from the dating stage to long-term commitment. **I'm going to walk you through the strategies you need to filter out bad matches. Believe me, this chapter will save you a lot of time**.

Communication skills are important in two respects in the early days of a relationship. First, you need to know how to let someone understand who you are and what you want. Second, you need to be able to read the signs that indicate someone isn't on the same page as you or, even worse, that they have serious emotional or psychological problems.

Are you really ready to date?

You might know all about great communication in theory, but if you don't have the right approach to dating, it won't get you very far. Before you look for a partner, ask yourself some questions.

Psychological research has shown that you absolutely must possess personal insight, the capacity for mutuality, and emotional regulation skills before you can even hope to enter into a good relationship.[6] Think of these questions as your preflight check:

Question 1: Do you have insight into your own feelings, and do you know what you really want from a partner?

There's no point in trying to find a partner if you don't even know what you want! Think about the kind of relationship you need, the qualities you want in a mate,

---

[6] TEDxTalks. (2015). *Skills for Healthy Romantic Relationships – Joanne Davila*. youtube.com

and what you can learn from past relationships. **If you are hazy on what you want, you'll waste time on people who aren't remotely suitable for you.** Self-knowledge and emotional intelligence are also vital for successful dating. Otherwise, when it comes to talking about your feelings, you'll find it hard to communicate with your partner.

Question 2: Are you willing to create a relationship based on mutuality?

Are you truly ready to get to know someone as they really are, and to compromise when the going gets tough? All relationships face problems. Using the techniques in this book, you'll be able to find solutions that work for both of you. However, you need a lot of emotional maturity if you are to meet someone halfway.

Question 3: Can you regulate your emotions?

Have you ever had a partner or friend who used you as their personal therapist? I have! My high school girlfriend, Savannah, was a great match for me in a lot of ways. We shared a few similar interests, had the same sense of humor, and we found each other very attractive.

The problem? Savannah had the habit of talking – at length – about all her problems, no matter how trivial, every single time we were together. Whether it was a math teacher who had given her a low grade, her annoying little brother who played his music too loudly, or a friend of hers who had started copying her fashion sense, she wanted to talk about it – for hours.

Savannah was just a teenager. Surely, she would have developed better communication skills in her twenties, right? Unfortunately, I've seen too many people in their thirties, forties (and beyond!) who never learned how to regulate their own emotions. For example, they come home from a hard day at work and get snappy with their partner. **It's immature, it's unhealthy, and it's a big turnoff.**

You need to tolerate uncomfortable emotions without taking them out on your partner. If you aren't in a position to do that, you shouldn't be looking for a relationship. Your priority, for the sake of your own mental health and that of your future partner, should be on developing your emotional intelligence (EQ) instead. Learn how to recognize your own emotions, and develop some healthy coping strategies.

Reading the signs – valuable communication skills that will see you through the early days of a relationship

Assuming you are ready for a relationship, it's time to move on to the strategies you should use when you start dating someone. Let's review what you need to achieve on the first two or three dates:

1) You want to make sure that your date is searching for a relationship;

2) You want to make sure that they are capable of healthy communication;

3) You want to screen your date for red flags;

4) You want to make sure that the two of you are not fundamentally incompatible.

I'm going to take these points one by one, and show you how to quickly establish whether it's worth trying to develop a lasting relationship with your date.

1. Is this person really in the market for a relationship?

I'm sure I don't need to tell you that the dating world is full of people who just want quick flings, people who are only dating in a bid to get over their ex-partners, and people who aren't sure what they want from a relationship.

It's inevitable that you'll come across a few of these types, but you can become skilled at spotting them. Of course, you can't expect to form a relationship after just one or two dates, but you can find out early on whether someone is searching for something meaningful.

Here's how to make sure that the two of you are on the same page:

Ask them insightful questions, and see whether they reciprocate: People who are looking for a meaningful relationship want to get to know their date. Once you've moved past the small talk stage, ask them a few questions about their favorite dreams and most treasured goals.

If they ask you a few similar questions in return – and seem interested in what you have to say – this is a positive sign. It's not a guarantee that they want a serious relationship, but it's a good start.

Be on guard for repeated references to physical intimacy: How can I put this nicely? Sometimes, great relationships do start with casual sex. However, someone who is looking for a long-term partner won't usually make it their mission to talk you into bed within the first couple of dates.

If your date seems particularly keen to hint at their sexual prowess, or keeps asking you about your "preferences," then they are probably only looking for one thing. Strange attitudes towards physical intimacy that are worlds apart from your own are also a big red flag, because someone who holds odd attitudes towards sex is likely to be dysfunctional in other areas too.[7]

Pay attention to any mention of ex-partners: All references to an ex should be brief, relevant, and positive. If they casually mention numerous ex-partners, this isn't a good sign. It suggests that they have poor judgment when it comes to relationships, that they get bored easily, or that they are afraid of commitment. Proceed with caution! One day, they might decide to talk about you in the same way. This can ruin your reputation.

Look out for references to future scenarios that aren't compatible with a relationship: When they talk about what they intend to do over the next few months, consider whether they have accounted for a serious relationship. For example, if they

---

[7] Lue, N. (2006). *Knowing When To Bail Out – Red Flags.* baggagereclaim.co.uk

tell you that they have just signed up to work for six months in a foreign country and that they leave in eight weeks' time, they probably aren't looking for a serious relationship.

If they have concrete plans that will take up a lot of their time in the near future, there's a quick and easy way to uncover their intentions: "That sounds exciting! I'm guessing it means you won't be looking for something too serious for a while, then?"

Ask questions that assess their overall outlook on life: Almost any question can be used to gauge your date's personality. For example, if you ask them what books they have read lately, a pessimistic person will seize the chance to give a scathing review, or at least to dwell on the parts they didn't like.

The most innocent of questions can reveal a lot about someone's personality. Even if they say that their goal is to find their soulmate, someone who is generally bitter and resentful when talking about everyday topics isn't ready for a mature relationship. Let them go! You just don't need that kind of negativity in your life.

Once you are in rapport, you can ask whether they are looking for a relationship: Under no circumstances should you open a date with a question about the other person's relationship goals, but there is nothing wrong with asking them later on if the date is going well.

If you don't feel able to ask them outright, take a subtler approach by asking them about their goals for the next five or ten years. If they are looking for a long-term relationship, they will usually take the chance to offer up the information. If not, say something like "No wife/husband and kids in there?" in a light-hearted way. Their response will tell you everything you need to know.

Guess what? If they tell you that they don't want a relationship, or that they "aren't the type to settle down," your job is to believe them and move on. Yes, there is a slim chance that they will change their mind when they realize how great you are, but it's a poor bet. Be smart and focus on someone who wants the same thing.[8]

2. Does this person have the ability to communicate in a healthy manner?

Try these tips to find out whether they have a history of good communication with other people, and whether they can handle everyday tension and conflict:

Ask them what kind of people they like to hang out with, or ask them to describe their closest friends: Psychological research backs up the "Birds of a feather flock together" cliché. Most people prefer to hang out with people similar to themselves.[9]

The scientific term for this is "social homophily." This means that if your date tells you stories that suggest their friends are unpleasant or have poor social skills, you should consider yourself warned.

Try to get a handle on what kind of relationship they have with their parents: As you will learn later in this book, children who have a secure, healthy relationship with their parents are more likely to have healthy relationships as adults. This doesn't mean that people with unhealthy family relationships cannot learn to become great communicators.

However, a troubled family background can be a warning sign if they haven't deliberately worked on their interpersonal skills. People who grew up with poor communicators as role models can find it hard to relate to others.[10]

Ask a few general questions about their family, and you will probably gain insight into the parent-child relationship. If they do not get on with their parents, they should be able to talk about the situation in a calm, straightforward way that suggests they have resolved any underlying resentment or grief.

---

[8] Ryan, R.A. (2016). *7 Signs They're Not Looking For A Real Relationship*. self.com
[9] McPherson, M., Smith-Lovin, L., & Cook, J.M. (2001). Birds Of A Feather: Homophily in Social Networks. *Annual Review Of Sociology, 27*, 415-44.
[10] Streep, P. (2014). *Why Your Partner May Be Like Your Parent*. psychologytoday.com

Again, I don't want you to write someone off just because their early childhood wasn't perfect. However, if they tell you that their family relationships were (or are) especially dysfunctional, proceed with caution.

Ask them about the kind of people they work with, and whether they like their colleagues: If they complain that no one at work likes them, or that they have had one bad boss after another, beware! When someone is the only common denominator across many difficult social situations, it is likely that they are deficient in the skills needed to form and maintain relationships.

Voice an opposing view and observe how they handle it: Don't disagree with your date for the sake of it, but if you happen to hold an opinion that differs from their own, then air it! Watch how they react.

Hopefully, they will accord you respect and empathy. If their response makes you uncomfortable, consider the possibility that they are unaccustomed to dealing with disagreements, which doesn't bode well for the long haul.

3. Are there any red flags?

Some red flags are obvious. If they are married, tell you that they struggle with an alcohol addiction, or haven't held down a job in years, it's time to bail. But what about signs that they aren't good communicators? Take a look at this list:

They can't say "sorry:" Someone who can't give an apology, or who distorts reality to serve their own ends, is to be avoided. At best, they may have a bad memory. At worst, they could be a sociopath who takes delight in manipulating other people. If you catch them in a lie, forget about seeing them again – how can you trust someone who is willing to deceive you so early on?

By the way, this doesn't just apply to big lies. If they tell you stories that don't quite add up, or if they contradict themselves at any point, it's probably time to drop them and move on.

Their communication is sporadic: Is your date lively and engaging one day, then cool or even ambivalent the next? If their energy levels ebb and flow for no apparent reason, it's time to back off. Someone who wants to impress you will be consistently attentive.

They talk a lot – but don't really say much of value: Have you ever walked away from what felt like a great date, only to realize that you hadn't learned much about the other person? Don't ignore this red flag, because it suggests that they have trouble sharing personal information with other people. If you suspect that they are hiding something, you are probably right.

They claim to have never been in love: If your date is well into adulthood (say, over the age of 30) and maintain that they have never been in love, tread carefully. Unless they have lived under a rock or in a rural commune, there's probably a good reason why they haven't managed to develop a close bond with someone else.

It feels as though every conversation is a minefield: When you can't hold an ordinary conversation with someone unless you tread carefully at all times, this suggests that they have never learned how to regulate their emotions or work through differences in opinion. They aren't a good relationship candidate, so back away fast!

They press for too much detail too soon, or they give you far too much information: If you have been on dates with people who seem aloof, a person who opens up within seconds can be a refreshing change. But watch out – people like this often have poor boundaries, and their inappropriate communication style suggests that they have no concept of privacy.

Someone who claims to love you after a couple of dates, or talks about marriage and children within the first few weeks, is probably bad news. People like this prefer fantasy over reality.[11] Steer clear!

These red flags don't necessarily mean that your date is a bad person. Sometimes, there is an innocent explanation for odd behavior.

---

[11] Lue, N. (2010) *Fast-forwarding: When Someone Speeds You Through Dating.* baggagereclaim.co.uk

For example, if someone is nervous and worried that they will not make a good impression, they might start rambling on about generic topics that don't encourage deep conversation.

However, you should think carefully before giving them the benefit of the doubt. You are not there to play the part of therapist. You deserve someone who is ready to date right now, not in some hypothetical future in which they have sorted out their issues.

4. Do you have any reason to suspect that the two of you are simply incompatible?

We've all been guilty of trying to overlook someone's faults just because we find them attractive, or because we are sick of being single and want to find a partner. It's human nature. Unfortunately, there are some points of incompatibility that are insurmountable.

Note that an incompatibility doesn't indicate that the other person is "bad," or that they couldn't be your friend, just that you are never going to work out as romantic partners. Your job, as an excellent communicator and emotionally mature adult, is to pick up on these problems early and handle them in a dignified manner.

Let me tell you a story. My friend Matt was on vacation last year. Whilst hanging out at the bar one evening, he met the woman of his dreams – or so he thought. I'll call her Sasha.

Over the next few days, Sasha and Matt spent almost every hour together. Matt discovered that she only lived two hours away from him, so there was a chance that they could continue their romance after the vacation was over. He couldn't believe his good luck!

On the last night of the trip, Matt made his move. He asked Sasha whether she would like to try dating once their vacation had ended. "Sure," Sasha said. "But of course, my daughter will always come first."

Matt was stunned. Why? Because in their six days together, Sasha had never thought to mention that she had a child. He backtracked fast, telling her that he didn't think it would be a good idea for them to carry on seeing one another.

Not only had Sasha demonstrated an ability to drip-feed someone the truth at a pace that suited her, but Matt had known for years that he never wanted children – a fact he had mentioned to Sasha during their first evening together.

When he told me this story, he looked sad and uncertain. "Was I too hasty?" he asked. "She was pretty much perfect otherwise, and maybe I could have grown to like the kid eventually."

Needless to say, Matt was not "too hasty." He's an emotionally mature guy who realized that Sasha's strange relationship with the truth would only set him up for pain in the long run.

He hasn't found the right woman yet, but I can tell you with 100% certainty that it wasn't Sasha. Poor communication skills, plus a key point of incompatibility (in this case, attitudes towards children), is a recipe for misery.

Whether it's politics, religion, attitudes to childrearing, or general perspectives on life, some differences should send you running in the opposite direction.

The difficult part is not so much identifying obvious differences, but in letting go of your hopes that this person could have been a perfect match for you. **However, keeping yourself rooted in reality is the only path to a healthy relationship.** Keep your eyes and ears open!

Chapter 2: Identifying & Handling Codependency

We seek relationships because we like to feel good about ourselves and, ideally, to make someone else feel good at the same time. Interdependency – a state of feeling connected to other people - is healthy and normal. Human society thrives on it.[12] If everyone chose to remain alone, we would never be able to collaborate on projects or nurture the next generation.

Hugging, touching, and being in a state of strong rapport generates feelings of pleasure and excitement, which encourages us to keep on seeking contact with others. We are literally made for relationships!

What is codependency?

Unfortunately, many of us don't go into romantic relationships willing and able to see a partner as our equal. Ideally, a relationship allows two separate people to meet and build a strong bond that respects both their identities.

You should feel secure in yourself as an individual, and respect your partner as their own person with their own set of needs, wants, and desires.

Sounds good, doesn't it? The trouble is, this kind of relationship requires a strong sense of self-esteem and self-reliance. Lots of us grow up in homes that don't encourage healthy interdependency.

Instead, we learn that relationships in which neither person is quite sure where they end and the other person begins are normal. If you are in a codependent relationship, you will always feel as though your emotions and personality overlap with those of your partner.

Uncovering codependency

---

[12] Lancer, D. (2016). *Codependency Vs. Interdependency.* psychcentral.com

If you are codependent, you will have a distinct style of relating to, and communicating with, other people. Here are a few helpful questions you can ask yourself as a kind of self-assessment:

Do you tend to "absorb" someone else's moods?: If you meet up with a friend or partner who seems sad or angry, does your own emotional state suddenly decline? Do you find it impossible to be calm or happy when you know or suspect that someone else isn't feeling good?

If you are codependent, you will find it hard to stay in touch with your own feelings. Instead, you automatically look to other people to help you "decide" how to feel. Codependent people take on responsibility for other peoples' emotions. If you feel compelled to make someone else's bad mood "right," you might well be codependent.[13]

Do you question your decisions and life direction when someone disagrees with you?: A sense of general indecisiveness and a willingness to change your plans if and when someone disagrees with you is a hallmark of codependency. Codependent people don't like conflict, and would rather go along with what someone else suggests that put forward their own suggestions.

Do you panic when someone even hints at leaving you?: Abandonment issues are a key element of codependency. Because a codependent feels "lost" without someone by their side, the prospect of someone ending a relationship is scary.

Do you try to control your partner's behaviors?: Codependent people rely on others to shore up their own sense of self, but this doesn't mean that they are always meek and mild. In fact, a lot of codependent people expend plenty of time and effort trying to change other people. Creating a sense of control helps them feel safe in a relationship.

Do you have trouble separating your partner's problems from your own?: If you assume that it's your job to control every area of your partner's life and solve all

---

[13] Ibid.

their problems, you are setting yourself up for a lot of stress. Worse, you'll be distracted from your own issues! If this sounds familiar, you are likely to be codependent.

Why do people become codependent?

There are two factors at play here. The first is a person's experience of childhood relationships. If an individual grows up in an unsafe home environment, they have had to draw on emotional survival tactics to keep themselves safe.

For example, someone who grew up with abusive parents might learn how to calm them down in the hope of reducing the risk of further abuse.[14]

Our most basic need is safety, so a child will do whatever it takes to feel secure. The problem starts when these patterns carry over into adulthood.[15] To continue with the example above, the child might grow into an adult who assumes that unless they keep everyone calm and happy, something terrible might happen.

The second factor is cultural pressures. Codependency is actively encouraged by Western culture. The phrases "other half" and "better half" are frequently tossed around in conversation.

They set up an expectation that when we get into a relationship, the other person will magically solve all our emotional and psychological problems. **This doesn't exactly encourage healthy, balanced relationships.**

In a healthy relationship, two self-defined people build a strong bond that enriches their lives. In a codependent relationship, two people do not build a relationship that joins two complete individuals together.

---

[14] Cole, T. (2016). *What is Codependency?* youtube.com
[15] Clark-Faler, E. (2012). *The Wounded Child, Adaptive Child & Functioning Adult.* recoveryhelpnow.com

Instead, they rely on each other for validation. Some codependent people want their partners to tell them how to live their lives, what to believe, and even how to conduct the relationships they have with their family and friends.[16]

Communication strategies for codependent people

Don't despair if you recognize yourself as a codependent person. With time and effort, you can change. You will need to approach your relationships in a new way – and this starts with your communication strategies.[17]

Start acknowledging that you have normal human needs: Codependent people often erect a façade in their relationships. They usually say that everything is fine, that they are perfectly content with the way things are, and that they are happy to put everyone else's needs before their own.

Putting on an act stops other people getting to know the real you, and it will also make you feel like a martyr. Instead, you need to start having authentic conversations. **If a partner or friend asks how you are feeling, tell them!** Let yourself be vulnerable by admitting that your life isn't perfect, and that you need help from time to time.

Stop expecting other people to read your mind!: Remember, in a codependent relationship, two people become so enmeshed that they start to feel as though their emotions and personalities are one and the same. In case you hadn't already figured it out, this is a ridiculous way to conduct a relationship.

No one can possibly know exactly what someone else is thinking at any given moment, and to believe otherwise is asking for trouble. Don't assume that someone who really loves you will magically know what you want and need. Stop making assumptions.

---

[16] Mellody, P., Wells Miller, A., & Miller, J.K. (2003). *Facing Codependence: What It Is, Where It Comes From, How It Sabotages Our Lives.* New York, NY: Harper & Row.
[17] Ibid.

Here's a classic example of how "mind reading" plays out in codependent relationships. Let's say that Kelly, a codependent woman, is in a relationship with a man called Jim. Jim realizes that Kelly's birthday is two weeks away, so he asks her what she would like as a gift.

Kelly tells him, "Whatever you get will be fine. I'm sure you'll choose well!" In her head, Kelly tells herself that Jim will probably get her the gold necklace she was admiring in a jeweler's window the last time they went shopping. She thinks, "He must have noticed that I really loved that necklace."

Jim, who takes Kelly at her word, goes to the mall and chooses a gift he thinks she will like – a silver bracelet with a heart-shaped charm. He picks out a card to go with his gift, and also decides to buy Kelly a box of gourmet chocolates.

Imagine his surprise when Kelly looks disappointed with his selection! He has no idea that he was supposed to read Kelly's mind, and Kelly can't understand why her partner failed to realize that she actually wanted the gold necklace.

A woman with no codependent tendencies would have told her partner that she wanted the necklace, because she would know that it's unrealistic to expect her partner's thoughts to somehow merge with her own.

Learn to assess someone's advice on its own merits: A codependent person finds it hard to stay true to their own decisions and values if someone disagrees with them. If this applies to you, it's time to start listening carefully to what other people say, and then disregarding their "advice" if it isn't helpful.

Don't assume that they are right! Ask questions like "Why do you think I should do that?," and "Do you have any other ideas?" Digging deeper will give you the bigger picture. Do not blindly trust in another person's judgment.

Stop offering unsolicited advice: Not only do you need to think twice before taking someone's suggestions on board, but you must also train yourself to stay out of other people's affairs. Unless you are asked for your input, hold back. I know, I know

– trying to take charge of a situation makes you feel safe. But you cannot have a balanced relationship unless you give the other person the freedom to make their own decisions (and their own mistakes).

Challenge judgments: Codependent people are scared of being judged, because they tend to assume that when someone criticizes them, the criticism is probably justified. They also assume that if someone criticizes them, then they are "bad" and might be abandoned as a result.

Neither assumption is true. To break out of codependency, you need to start asking whether the person judging you is objectively correct, or just voicing their opinion. Think like a journalist – consider the source! As you build up your own self-esteem and identity, you will start to care less about what others think.

Identify and stop passive-aggressive communication: When you don't feel as though you have the right to voice your true needs, you might pretend that everything is OK whilst secretly dwelling on your problems.

The trouble with resentment is that you can't keep it hidden forever – it can and will rise to the surface. This pattern of behavior, commonly known as "passive-aggressive communication," is harmful to relationships.

I'll address assertive communication later in this book, but for now, start thinking about how you can begin to say what you really mean rather than what you think others want to hear.

Focus on individuals, not outcomes: Codependency is exhausting. A codependent individual will pour their energy into imposing their will on their partner, rather than truly listening and learning what the other person needs.

Instead of having the courage to have an authentic conversation, they are attached to an outcome. They treat their partners as players in a hypothetical situation, not as fellow humans with their own needs and free will.

Freeing yourself from codependency means letting go of your need to control people, and instead focus on reaching agreements that work for both of you. Good listening skills, a willingness to accept reality, and conflict resolution strategies will all help here.

The ultimate tool for codependent people

The above strategies will help you build healthier relationships and work towards interdependency rather than codependency. However, there's one tool I've left off the list.

Overcoming codependency relies on the separation between yourself and other people, and the behaviors you will and won't tolerate from those around you. In therapy circles, this is referred to as "setting boundaries."

Without boundaries, you will never have a good relationship, because you will feel responsible for other people's actions and feelings along with your own. Boundaries are so important that the next chapter is devoted to the topic! Turn the page and learn how to stand up for yourself, no matter what the situation.

Chapter 3: Setting & Defending Boundaries In A Relationship

A boundary is the psychological equivalent of a fence. To lay down a boundary is to tell others that they must not engage in a particular behavior and, if they insist on doing so, that there will be consequences. The art of setting and defending boundaries relies on strong self-esteem and good communication skills.

Self-esteem allows you to decide what (and who) you will and won't tolerate in your life, and your communication skills help you hold others accountable if they try to trample on your rights.

When people don't know how to use their words to communicate boundaries, they will use unhealthy strategies instead. These tactics include screaming, shouting, and withdrawal. As you can imagine, this approach hardly makes for good relationships! In this chapter, I'll teach you how to keep your boundaries intact in a calm, dignified manner.

Why are boundaries so vital for a healthy relationship?

If you are not used to standing up for yourself, the concept of boundaries might make you uneasy at first. Those who are used to putting everyone else's needs ahead of their own can feel as though upholding personal boundaries is selfish. This is completely untrue.[18]

Believe it or not, establishing your boundaries will benefit the people in your life. As a rule, human beings respect those who stand firm in their convictions, act in a predictable manner, and know their own self-worth.

If you have children or manage other people as part of your job, setting and defending boundaries will make you a positive role model. Working on your boundaries won't make everyone like you, but it will make you less of a target for bullies and negative people.

---

[18] Barregar, C. (2016). *Is Setting Healthy Boundaries An Act Of Selfishness Or Love?* goodmenproject.com

Choosing your boundaries

It's up to you to set your own boundaries. We all have different tastes, preferences, and personalities. For example, I'm open to hearing other people's life stories.

I'm also happy to share some personal information quite early on in a relationship, because that has always felt natural and normal to me. However, I have a few friends who prefer to keep their personal lives private until they have had a chance to build up trust with a new acquaintance.

This means that my boundaries around sharing personal information are quite relaxed – you have to push me pretty far before I tell you to stop asking me questions - whereas my friends' boundaries are stricter.

For instance, they wouldn't be happy talking about their health problems unless they already had a bond with their conversation partner, so if the issue came up early on, they would quickly let the other person know that the topic was off limits.

Neither approach is "right" or "wrong." As long as you have the self-awareness to choose boundaries that work for you, and the skills needed to communicate these boundaries, you'll be just fine.

If you aren't sure what your boundaries are, think about the following:

Physical boundaries: These relate to physical proximity and touch. For example, some people are perfectly happy to hug friends and acquaintances, whereas others prefer to keep their distance.

Someone with appropriate personal boundaries knows how to stop others from touching them inappropriately, and can make their own decisions when it comes to social contact such as kissing and hugging.

Think about what makes you feel uncomfortable, and the boundaries you might want to set. For instance, you may not want to hug someone unless they are a close friend who has been in your life for a long time. "I don't hug people unless I know them very well. Being forced to do so is unacceptable to me" would be a useful boundary in this case.

Emotional boundaries: How far do you allow someone else's emotions to influence your own? Do you have clear boundaries around how often other people can share their deepest feelings with you?

When you have strong emotional boundaries, you stop acting as a sponge for other people's feelings. You can draw a line between yourself and another person. In other words, you stop being codependent!

If you find yourself acting as an energy dump for other people and it's bringing you down, it's time to set some boundaries. For instance, you might decide that you will not engage in any negative conversations with anyone after 9pm in the evening, because you need to wind down in preparation for work the next day.

"I do not answer my phone after 9pm, unless it's an emergency" would be a suitable boundary in this particular situation.

Communication boundaries: These boundaries concern the ways in which someone addresses you, and the language they use. "I will not permit someone to shout at me," and "I will not allow someone to mock me" are two great examples of communication boundaries.[19]

Sticking to your emotional boundaries protects you against manipulation. When someone is able to make you feel guilty for no good reason, you are vulnerable to emotional blackmail.

---

[19] Fulcher, K. (2003). *Speak Up For Yourself: Create and Communicate Boundaries.* wahm.com

When you have the ability to tell someone that their feelings are not your responsibility, they might not like it – but they will no longer have a hold over you. This is true emotional freedom!

Some of your boundaries might be flexible, whereas others will be nonnegotiable. For example, you may decide that if a friend drinks heavily or takes illegal drugs, you will leave their home – no exceptions.

On the other hand, you might be more flexible when it comes to working occasional overtime at the office. It's up to you! The important thing is that you get comfortable with letting others know your limits.[20]

Words and phrases that set out your boundaries

So let's get down to it – what are the magic words that establish boundaries? Here's how to talk to someone who tries to violate your physical or emotional space:

Use "I" statements: When you share your own perspective (e.g. "I need you to stop...") rather than pass judgment on what someone else is doing or thinking (e.g. "You always..."), you are less likely to receive pushback.

After all, someone can argue that your interpretation of their own emotional state is wrong, but no one can deny that you know your own thoughts and feelings.

Do not use euphemisms: When laying down a boundary, call a spade a spade. Don't dance around someone else's bad behavior. For example, if they have used obscene or insulting language around you, don't tell them that their words "aren't nice." Spell it out.

It would be better to say, "Your language is offensive to me and makes me feel uncomfortable. I do not want to listen to it. If you continue to talk like that, I will leave the room."

---

[20] Hill, M. (2017). *Setting Boundaries: How to Draw the Line When You Have No Idea Where to Put it.* lifehack.org

If possible, open with a positive statement: If you think the other person is coming from a place of positive intentions and has made an honest mistake in overstepping a boundary, opening with a compliment or piece of praise can set the right tone.

For example, if you are about to explain that you don't like to hug people, you could start by acknowledging that you appreciate their desire to show you how much they care.

Use the five-point structure: Professional coach and author Kimberly Fulcher recommends a five-step approach[21] to stating a boundary:

1. Begin by outlining what the problem is.

2. Tell the other person what, precisely, is unacceptable about their behavior.

3. Tell them how their behavior makes you feel.

4. Ask them to implement a solution that will stop future boundary violations.

5. Tell them what the consequences will be if they do not respect your request.

For instance, if your colleague keeps borrowing your office equipment without permission, you need to lay down a clear boundary such as the following:

"I've noticed that you keep borrowing my equipment without asking permission. This isn't acceptable because it means I can't get my work done. This makes me feel frustrated and anxious about my deadlines. Please ask in future before borrowing any equipment. If you do not, I will have to lock it away in my draw, or make a formal complaint against you."

---

[21] Fulcher, K. (2003). *Speak Up for Yourself: Create and Communicate Boundaries.* wahm.com

Sharpen your conflict management skills: When you know that you can deal with rejection, disagreements, and even the threat of abandonment, you will find it easier to defend your boundaries. You'll feel more comfortable interacting with other people when you can trust yourself to react appropriately to whatever they say or do.[22]

Do not apologize: Remember – everyone is entitled to their own boundaries, and this includes you! Never say sorry for valuing yourself. Other people have no right to treat you like a second-class citizen, and enforcing your boundaries is a sign of great mental health. If someone else can't handle that, it's their issue.

Match your actions and body language to your words: No one deserves to be treated poorly, but if you show via your actions that your boundaries do not matter, people won't take you seriously.

For example, if you tell your partner that you need them to take responsibility for half of the housework, yet you still tidy up after them, you are communicating via your actions that you don't really mean what you say. After all, your behavior hasn't changed!

Identify and prepare for difficult situations: Think about common situations that make you feel uncomfortable, and practice saying the right words that will lay down your boundaries. For example, it's a good idea to decide on a statement to use when you need to buy yourself time to think.[23]

Some people have the unpleasant habit of putting others on the spot and demanding an instant answer to an awkward question. Be prepared by coming up with an effective way of implementing a boundary. "I cannot answer that right now. I will take time to think and get back to you in an hour" is a sensible response.

---

[22] OWN. (2015). *Advice That Will Change the Way You See Every Relationship*. youtube.com
[23] Clarke University. (2017). *Setting Personal Boundaries*. clarke.edu.

Consistency is essential

Emotionally intelligent people will respect your boundaries. Of course, I realize that there are a lot of people out there who still have some work to do in that department. From time to time, you will come up against people who will try to ignore your boundaries. There are only two ways to remedy this.

The first is to remain strong and consistent. Repeat your boundary statement more than once if necessary, using a clear tone of voice. If they still don't respect your wishes, it's time to impose consequences.

Remember, you should have set them out in your original boundary statement. It is absolutely essential that you follow through, because if you back down, people will think that you are weak.

I work with a lot of clients who struggle to set boundaries. When I walk them through the five-step process, they react with horror. They tell me that they "couldn't possibly do that," or that they "aren't assertive enough." Nonsense. Anyone can set boundaries.

Yes, it takes practice. Yes, it will feel uncomfortable at first. But is it a learnable skill? Definitely! Make a commitment to implementing the advice in this chapter, and you'll soon start to enjoy your relationships a whole lot more.

Chapter 4: Defining A Relationship

Once you've been dating someone for a while, the next step is to move from the "getting to know you" stage to the "relationship stage." It's often easier said than done! Some people will tell you that if a relationship is destined to work out, you won't need to have "the talk."

It's true that some couples make the transition seamlessly, but sometimes both parties get confused about what the other person wants and needs. The good news is that, if you prepare yourself for any possible outcome, you can handle "the talk" with dignity and grace.

How the typical dating situation unfolds

Does this story sound familiar? You meet someone you really like, and you go on a few dates. Perhaps you start sleeping with them. Within a few weeks, you realize that you would like to get into a relationship with this person, and your feelings are reciprocated – or are they?

It's amazing how rapidly we can find ourselves wondering whether that special person is seeing someone else, whether they see a future with us, and whether they like us as much as we like them.[24] As the weeks go by, that urge to know where the relationship is heading starts to grow stronger and stronger.

At this point, you have to make a choice. When it comes down to it, you only have two options:

Continue with the relationship, hoping that they will raise the issue: This can prolong the agony. Choosing to ride it out seems like the easy option at first, but you'll start to drive yourself mad pretty quick.

---

[24] Boundless. (2017). *DTR Assessment.* boundless.com

With every day that passes, you'll become increasingly obsessed with what they are thinking, when they are going to make it official, and so on. Your behavior and attitude will probably change, and the other person will wonder what's on your mind. Needless to say, I really don't recommend this option.

Ask them what they want from the relationship: This is a much better strategy, because it is transparent and authentic. As long as you plan the conversation carefully, you stand a good chance of getting the answers you need.

Ideally, you will have a strong rapport with the other person, and you will feel able to ask them direct questions. However, I realize that in some situations, it might be best to take a gentler approach or frame your question in a more casual way.

Why it's such a hard discussion to have

We don't want to appear desperate: There is a lot of pressure on both sexes to avoid appearing too needy or desperate.[25] There's some logic to this – not many people want to spend time with a clingy partner, and confidence is always attractive. The downside is that when both people are determined to play it cool, a stalemate situation develops. Both parties are left wondering what the heck is going on.

We think we already know the answer, and we don't like it: Sometimes your gut will be telling you that someone isn't really interested in a relationship, but you would rather remain in a state of denial than face the truth. It's natural to try and avoid the pain of rejection, but here's the thing – you will have to come back down to earth at some point anyway.[26]

Even if you manage to avoid "the talk" for several months, the very fact that neither of you are willing to communicate about your relationship will tell you everything you need to know. The truth will smack you in the face one way or the other, so why not do it on your own terms?

---

[25] Stanley, S.M. (2014). *3 Reasons Why People Avoid Talking About "The Relationship."* psychologytoday.com
[26] Ibid.

I've been guilty of ignoring my gut before. A few years ago, I met a woman – I'll call her Zoe - through a mutual friend. She and I had been on only six dates before I started daydreaming the fantastic relationship ahead of us.

Zoe didn't often reply to my texts, she didn't call me, and I always had to arrange our dates. Looking back, I can see that I was in serious denial, but at the time she seemed so chatty and happy on our dates that I told myself it didn't matter. I decided that if everything went well for two months, I would ask whether she wanted to make the relationship official.

A couple of weeks later, I was talking to my friend Michelle about the situation. She listened to me ramble on for a few minutes, and then frowned. Michelle is normally an upbeat, optimistic person, so I was surprised by her reaction.

"I don't think you're going to like what I have to say," Michelle said. "But you're telling me that unless the two of you are actually on a date, this lady doesn't bother with you. If I had to place a bet, I don't think she'll take you up on the offer of a relationship." I bristled, and changed the subject.

Unfortunately, I ignored Michelle's warning and charged ahead with the relationship. At the two-month mark, I told Zoe that I always had a great time with her, and that it seemed like we were heading into girlfriend and boyfriend territory.

As soon as the words, "Shall we make it official?" were out of my mouth, I knew that Michelle had been right. Zoe said that she was sorry, but that she wasn't looking for a relationship.

It was a painful experience, but it taught me the importance of listening to my gut. But here's the key lesson – it could have been so much worse. If I had chickened out and not asked her at all, I might have spent months trying to win her over, only to watch her start dating another guy.

Tips that will make the talk easier

Whether you plan to ask someone directly or take a subtler route, here's what you should know before initiating the conversation:

It's essential that you do it face to face: Under no circumstances should you attempt to have such an important conversation over email, text, or even the phone. You need to be able to see their body language and facial expressions. I know it's scary, but you really can't afford to break this rule.

It's often easiest to say what you feel, then finish with a question: Don't open with a formal question. Sitting down and blurting "So, can we be official?" is a bit clumsy.

Instead, broach the topic by telling them what you have noticed or experienced in your time together so far. Then you can tag the sentence with a question that invites them to agree or disagree. For example:

"So over the past few weeks, we've been spending a lot of time together. It feels like we're in a relationship sometimes. Do you think it's heading that way?"

"I'm having such a good time getting to know you. I'd love us to try dating exclusively if you'd be open to that?"

If they feel the same way, they'll help you out: Practice what you're going to say, but don't worry too much about messing it up. If they return your feelings, they will jump at the chance to tell you.

The other person might be intimidated by the prospect of talking about the issue, even if they want a relationship: You'll notice that the openers above are brief. Always get to the point as soon as possible. The moment they sense that you are building up to an important question, they will start to wonder whether you are about to drop some bad news. Don't leave them in suspense!

It's best to have the conversation with no advance warning: Don't tell them beforehand that you have "something to talk about." This might put them on the defensive, and it creates a power imbalance. By leaving a gap between the warning and the actual event, you are leaving them hanging. This isn't fair, and it doesn't build trust.

You need to shut up and listen if they try to interrupt: There is a chance that the other person will have thought about this conversation too, and they might have planned their response in advance.

If they start talking, let them finish! They may be trying to open up about their feelings, and it's in your best interest to be quiet and listen.[27]

It's not a good idea to have the talk too soon: Clarifying your relationship status too soon will sound alarm bells for most people. Talking about your status after just a few weeks isn't normally a good idea.

You can't make an informed decision until you've had a chance to get to know them, so don't dive in too quickly. If in doubt, the three-month rule works in most cases.

You must know your wants and needs: There is nothing wrong with wanting a committed, monogamous relationship. There is nothing wrong with wanting an open relationship, either.

You get my point – people have all kinds of preferences, and no one has the right to make you feel bad for knowing what you want. Problems arise when we get so desperate for someone to like us that we accept their terms and conditions even if they don't meet our needs.

No matter how much you like someone, don't settle. Don't force yourself to accept what they're offering if it doesn't match your personal relationship goals.[28] Respect yourself enough to move on and find someone who is a better fit.

---

[27] Hudspeth, C. (2014). *When And How To Have That Awkward "Defining The Relationship" Talk.* thoughtcatalog.com

[28] eHarmony. (2016). *15 Ways To Have A Successful "Define The Relationship" Talk.* eharmony.com

Prepare for a negative response: Always know how you intend to respond if they don't tell you what you want to hear. It's not always easy to predict in advance how you will feel in response to a rejection, so think of a phrase that buys you a few minutes' breathing space if you find yourself crying or unable to think straight:

"It's OK, I just need a moment, don't worry."

"I'll be fine, I guess I'm just disappointed."

"Can I just step outside for a moment? I'll be right back."

Once you have regained your composure, thank them for being honest. Your thanks should be sincere – although rejection hurts, you will at least know where you stand. Thank them for the time you've spent together, and tell them that you have enjoyed getting to know them.

Unless the person rejecting you is a total jerk, they won't think you are weak or pathetic for showing your disappointment. (If they are a jerk about it, then you just dodged a bullet!) It takes courage to risk romantic rejection, so they will always remember you as a guy or girl who was willing to put themselves on the line. That's hardly a bad impression to leave.

Always make sure that they can leave without difficulty if the conversation goes wrong: For example, it's not a good idea to have the discussion at midnight on the couch after a romantic evening in. Choose a more neutral location. Having the conversation in a park or quiet corner of a coffee shop allows you to part ways quickly if it doesn't go well.

If they aren't sure, give them more time: Don't panic if your partner can't tell you precisely what they want or need at that moment in time. They may need some time to think before committing to a relationship. That's OK, but don't let them leave you hanging. Ask them to give you more details within a few days.

After a rejection, it's best to cut contact for a while: Don't kid yourself that you can immediately move from romantic rejection to friendship. It's emotional suicide.[29] Sure, you might form a friendship in the future, but it's only going to work if you can think of them with someone else without wanting to cry.

You don't have to play games here. Tell them how you feel, and let them know that you can't be buddies in the foreseeable future.

Be warned – some people will feel guilty at having caused you pain, and insist that the two of you stay in contact as "friends." For the reasons I've just outlined, this won't work. Look after your emotional health and maintain your boundaries.

---

[29] Lue, N. (2013). *The No Contact Rule.* London, England: Naughty Girl Media.

Chapter 5: Your Partner's Most Important Need, & How to Meet It

Relationships end for many reasons, but there is one major risk factor that people don't often talk about. We all know that a lack of trust, incompatible worldviews and the stress of significant life events can be enough to tear even the most loving couples apart, but what's the most lethal risk of all? Threats of abandonment.

Specifically, whenever you or a partner threaten to leave the relationship, it places a strain on the bond between you. In this chapter, I'll reveal exactly why this happens.

You'll learn why the threat of being abandoned is such a trigger point for so many people, and how you can build trust. In short, your partner's number one need in a relationship is a sense of trust and security. Ignore it at your peril.

Why fighting is inevitable

Some people mistakenly believe that if a couple fights, it must mean that they are incompatible. However, it's not arguments *per se* that drive a couple apart, but how secure they feel in the relationship. Another belief we need to rethink is the idea that arguments develop simply when beliefs and ideas clash.

That's true – but only to a point. Stan Tatkin, a researcher and therapist who specializes in communication, believes that neurobiology can help us understand why some relationships fall apart.

We need to look beyond what we talk about or do with our partners, and think about what happens in our primal (or "animal") brains when we interact with others.[30]

You don't need to be a neuroscientist to understand the basic functions of the brain. To put it simply, the "higher" parts of the brain - those areas visible on the

---

[30] TEDxTalks. (2016). *Relationships Are Hard, But Why? Stan Tatkin.* youtube.com

surface and positioned towards the front - are responsible for conscious thought. They allow us to rationalize, plan, and make deliberate judgments.[31]

The rest of the brain, sometimes referred to as the "lower" or "primitive" brain, runs on autopilot. It also alerts us to threats. You can think of it as your threat detection system. It allows you to react appropriately to danger.

Note that we aren't just talking about physical danger here. Our lower brain also allows us to react quickly to an emotional or psychological threat. For example, when someone says something that makes us mad, we move from "neutral" to "angry" in an instant.

The lower brain is responsible for automating your habits and routines. If you learn how to play the piano, drive a car, or perform any other skill that requires that you repeat a set of physical movements over and over again, your lower brain lays down "procedural memories."

Whenever you use that skill, your higher brain won't have to put in any effort. You can respond appropriately without having to sit down and think about what you are doing.[32]

Love becomes an automatic process

When you first meet someone and start dating, your conscious mind spends hours analyzing what they say, how they are acting, and whether or not the two of you are compatible. Your higher brain fixates on the other person. It wants to get to know them inside and out. The hormonal changes that take place in the brain and the rest of the body actively support this state of obsession.

For example, the serotonin levels in your brain drop, which encourages you to seek out the other individual as a source of happiness. Testosterone levels also change – the average man's testosterone levels decrease when he falls in love, whereas a

---
[31] Nature. (2017). *Prefrontal cortex.* nature.com
[32] Zimmermann, K.A. (2014). *Procedural Memory: Definition and Examples.* livescience.com

woman's testosterone levels go up! Scientists aren't yet sure why this is, but we know for certain that love changes our body chemistry.[33]

However, even the strongest crushes eventually fade. As time goes on and we start to become comfortable with a partner, we tend to fall into a routine. They are no longer quite so exciting, because we know them well.

Or rather, we think we know them. This is totally natural. We can't afford to spend all our lives in a state of romantic obsession, because we'd never get anything else done!

Feeling comfortable isn't the issue here. The problems start when two people take one another for granted, and assume that they can tell what their partner is thinking. The relationship starts to run on autopilot, and one or both partners start to pay less attention to what the other person is actually saying and doing.

The result? Misunderstandings and arguments, of course! If you've ever been in a fight that seemed to come from nowhere and escalated fast, this will sound familiar.

Couples who have been together for a while will start to use phrases like "You always...," "You never...," and "We always...." These generalizations are annoying and make the situation worse. They set the stage for arguments!

Why couples threaten each other with abandonment

When you fight with someone, your mind and body become attuned to potential threats. Your lower brain kicks in, flooding your body with adrenalin and cortisol, which give you that "fight or flight" response. In the heat of the moment, it becomes hard to think rationally.

---

[33] Marazziti, D., & Canale, D. (2004). Hormonal changes when falling in love. *Psychoneuroendocrinology, 29, 7,* 931-6.

It doesn't take long before you become focused on how angry or upset you feel rather than the issue that started the fight in the first place! Emotions rise, tempers flare, and it becomes all too easy to make threats like:

"I've had enough! I can't be bothered with this relationship anymore!"

"Well, if you're so upset, maybe I'll just leave you alone!"

"I'm sick of fighting all the time, I'm done!"

Both parties can end up screaming and shouting as their nervous systems go into overdrive.[34] It feels good to make a threat at the time, but the long-term effects can ruin a relationship. Not only do threats undermine trust – it's hard to put your faith in someone who has a history of threatening to leave you – but it also lays a foundation for future fights.

For example, if you repeatedly threaten to leave your partner, they might start to bring this up in the future as a reason why they cannot talk to you about their problems.

Why are abandonment threats such a big deal?

At this point, you might be wondering why we are so sensitive to the possibility that a partner is thinking of leaving us. Here's a quick explanation. Our attitudes towards attachment and abandonment begin in early childhood.

When we are babies, we are totally dependent on other people to look after us. If a baby's caregiver (usually their mother) doesn't show him or her consistent love and affection, the baby becomes very anxious.

On some level, they know that if they are to survive, their caregiver must be motivated to provide food, warmth, and shelter. Abandonment literally equals death

---
[34] Paul, M. (2017). *Fight or Flight in Relationship Conflict.* huffingtonpost.com

if you are a baby. Although we can take care of ourselves as adults, we never fully shed our need for secure, safe relationships.

In a healthy parent-child relationship, the baby develops a secure attachment style. This means that the child will feel a strong bond with their parent. They will miss them when they are away, but they don't suffer too much because they feel sure that the parent loves them, and that they will return.

On the other hand, if a parent doesn't give their baby consistent love and attention, their child will grow up with a lot of relationship anxiety. A psychologist would say that they have an "insecure attachment style."[35]

Although all of us find abandonment scary to some degree, people with an insecure attachment style find it hard to trust others. They will often assume that everyone will leave at some point. For these people, threats of abandonment are particularly hard to take.

Studies with young adults show that the quality of the relationships they had with their parents shapes their attitudes towards romantic relationships later in life.

Basically, those who always felt safe and loved as children feel more confident in their adult relationships, whereas those who had challenging relationships with their parents tend to fear abandonment and look towards their partner for a sense of validation. They are also more likely to experience higher levels of negative emotions, and they feel less committed to their partners.[36]

What does this research show us? Basically, you will never kick the "need" for safety and security, because the human brain will always run according to primitive instinct and habit.

---

[35] Murphy, B., & Bates, G.W. (1997). Adult Attachment Style and Vulnerability To Depression. *Personality and Individual Differences, 22, 6,* 835-844.
[36] Simpson, J.A. (1990). Influence of Attachment Styles on Romantic Relationships. *Journal of Personality and Social Psychology, 59, 5,* 971-980.

Even as adults, we want to know that the people we love aren't going to suddenly walk out on us – and this is an even bigger worry if we didn't have a good early relationship with our primary caregiver. Create trust and stability in your relationship, and you will have a much better chance of staying together.

How to promote trust and stability in your relationship

Never use the threat of leaving as leverage: If you know that your partner is afraid of being abandoned – and that applies to most of us – it's tempting to use threats as a way of gaining control in a situation.

For example, if your partner wants to talk about an issue you would rather leave unexamined, saying something like "It's arguments like this that make me question our relationship" will encourage them to keep quiet.

This strategy is effective in the short term, but eventually your partner will become sick of you resorting to threats as a way of shutting down a difficult conversation. **Never resort to this tactic.** If you spot it in your partner, it's time to draw a boundary and let them know that it isn't acceptable.

Always fight face to face: Eye contact is essential for good communication. We convey so much of our meaning via our facial expressions. This is why you should not argue over the phone, via text message, or when sitting side by side in the car.

Wait until you can sit or stand face to face before tackling sensitive issues. We usually trust someone more if they make eye contact with us, and so face to face contact is likely to inspire more confidence in your relationship.

Don't respond immediately if your partner threatens to leave: Do you tend to react strongly the moment your partner says anything that upsets or shocks you? The next time you argue, break the cycle. Rather than escalating the situation by making a threat of your own or raising your voice, take a different approach.

Change your position, take a deep breath and ask for a moment to collect your thoughts. Ask a question that will help you better understand your partner's position. Remember that threats are often made when the lower brain is in control. If a fight has reached this point, it's time to take a break and continue the discussion later.

Remember that your partner's attachment style is important: As you know, some people experience situations in childhood that result in a secure attachment style, whereas others develop a tendency to form insecure attachments with others. In short, you and your partner might have different requirements when it comes to reassurance.

For some people, a single brief reminder that you love them and want to work through a problem is enough. Others need to be told repeatedly – especially when tensions are running high – that they are not being abandoned.

Of course, if you have a partner who is unusually clingy or worried about being left alone, it's their responsibility to sort out their own issues.

Deep down, even the most confident person wants to know where they stand in the eyes of others. We all know on an intuitive level that the best relationships are built on a shared sense of trust and equality.

In the next chapter, I'll show you another set of strategies that will help you and your partner recognize one another as equals.

Chapter 6: How to Make Assertive Communication Work In Your Relationships

Given that you are reading this book, it's a safe bet that you have an interest in communication and relationship skills. You've probably heard about the most common communication styles we use in our relationships[37]:

Passive communication: Passive communicators do not voice their thoughts or feelings. They put the needs of other people ahead of their own. Other people often think of them as doormats.

Aggressive communication: Those with an aggressive style of communication value their own needs above everyone else's, and they aren't afraid to show it! They are more successful in getting what they want compared to a passive communicator, but they may be known as a bully or loudmouth.

Passive-aggressive communication: When someone suppresses their true thoughts and feelings but communicates them in "subtle" ways, they are using passive-aggressive communication. For example, if someone agrees to do a job they don't really want to do, they might indirectly show their resentment by "accidentally" doing it wrong.

Assertive communication: Assertive communication is about balancing your own needs with those of everyone else. Assertive people know how and when to compromise, and they can keep their emotions in check when it comes to handling difficult situations.

Obviously, assertive communication is the most constructive of all the styles. Assertive people respect both themselves and others. They are direct, confident, and they don't play mind games.

---

[37] Violence Intervention and Prevention Center. (n.d.) *The Four Basic Styles Of Communication.* uky.edu

The Five-Step Model

Here's an excellent five-step model that will help you communicate assertively with your partner. (It also works well with friends, relatives, and colleagues.) It's a simple process that allows you to share your feelings, minimize the risk of conflict, and lay the groundwork for healthy collaboration.

The process:[38]

Step 1 – Using factual, concise statements, express your thoughts on the issue without becoming overly emotional. There's nothing wrong with strong emotions, but getting too angry or upset will trigger the other person's threat sensor.

They will then become defensive, and won't be receptive to what you need to say. Stick to one issue at a time. Check that your partner has understood what you have said by asking "Do you understand what I mean?," or "Do you need me to word this differently?"

Step 2 – Accord the other person the respect you would like to receive. Do not interrupt. Summarize what you think they just told you. "You think X because Y, is that right?" is a simple, effective way of letting them know that you have understood their view (or not).

At this stage in the process, you may find that the person you are dealing with is reluctant to open up to you. This might be because they are intimidated by your confidence, or it may be because they lack faith in their own convictions.

The best way of encouraging them to open up is via the use of questions. Start off by using questions that require very little effort to answer. Closed questions that only require a "Yes" or "No" answer, or questions that can be answered in just a couple of words, are effective here.

---

[38] Thompson, J. (2011). *5 Steps to Better Relationships Using Assertive Communication.* youtube.com

For instance, you could ask, "Do you agree that we should do X?" or "Do you want to go to Event A or Event B?" These are low-effort questions. Once they have started talking and appear a little more relaxed, you can start asking longer questions that invite more complicated responses.

Be patient with insecure and passive communicators. They usually appreciate some extra time in which to gather their thoughts. If you rush in and demand that they answer you immediately, they will shut down even further.

On the other hand, if you give them the space they need, they will slowly begin to trust you. In time, the conversations you have with them should become easier.

On other occasions, you might have to deal with someone who prefers to use an aggressive style of communication. Boundaries are an essential tool here. An aggressive person will see any sign of weakness or passivity as an invitation to carry on imposing their will.

Use your boundaries to spell out the consequences of their aggressive behavior, and follow through as necessary. For example, here are some boundaries you can use when dealing with an aggressive communicator:

"It is unacceptable for you to shout at me. It makes me feel uneasy. If you cannot speak at a reasonable volume, I will end this conversation."

"I do not tolerate people insulting me. It makes me feel belittled. Unless you stop insulting me right now, I will lodge a formal complaint."

"I will not accept you reeling off my supposed faults, given that they have no relevance to this conversation. If you cannot stick to the topic at hand, I am going to leave the room."

Another important tip when dealing with an aggressive communicator is to concentrate on generating proactive responses rather than taking on a reactive role.

For instance, if someone is berating you for your lack of participation in a team project, returning with a criticism of your own will only exacerbate the situation.

Instead, you should take a proactive approach and outline a couple of potential solutions. Aggressive people are more likely to accord you some respect once they realize that you intend to stand your ground and defend your boundaries.[39]

Do not attempt to placate them by suggesting that you can empathize with them, or that you understand their anger. They are likely to respond by telling you that you cannot possibly understand their position! Don't waste your breath by telling them that you relate to their emotions, or that you once found yourself in a similar situation.

Along with those who are openly hostile, you will sometimes have to deal with people who express their anger in a subtler manner. Passive-aggressive people are harder to spot than someone who uses direct aggression.

Signs of passive-aggressive behavior include a mismatch between someone's words and body language (which hints at deceit and manipulation), subtle sarcasm, a tendency to dodge questions and change the course of the conversation to something irrelevant, a habit of punishing people by using the silent treatment, and spreading negative gossip. Passive-aggressive people are sullen and slow to cooperate.

Passive-aggressive people want to trigger a strong reaction in another person and get away with it. They aren't concerned with actually solving a problem – they just want to assert their power without resorting to overt aggression.

The trick is to stay very calm, and ignore their immature behaviors. Think of them as a teenager who hasn't developed the skills they need to function in the adult world.

There is no point in getting mad with a teenager, or trying to use passive aggression in return. You should apply the same principles when dealing with passive-aggressive adults.

---

[39] Ni, P. (2014). *How to Negotiate With Difficult and Aggressive People.* psychologytoday.com

Stick to the facts. Don't fall into the trap of asking, "What's wrong?" when they shrug their shoulders or start pouting. (Yes, I have known passive-aggressive adults who pout.) When you give them the attention they crave, this acts as positive reinforcement and just encourages future passive-aggressive behavior.[40]

Step 3 – Now that you have both made your views known, you can start to work on conflict resolution and compromise. The best way to begin is to ask, "What can we agree on here?" Both of you will have needs that you are trying to meet. You will also both have fears.

This is true even in situations that seem pretty benign. For example, let's say you and your partner are arguing about how much money you will spend on your annual vacation. You want to go on a cheap vacation, whereas they seem intent on blowing your joint savings on an expensive cruise.

If you focused on what you could both agree on, you may discover that you both want to spend quality time together, to make great memories, and to have a relaxing week away from work.

Finding points of agreement builds a sense of trust and security, which in turn makes it more likely that your partner will listen. You could then talk about your fears. In your case, you might fear running out of money and not having a "buffer" to see you through an unexpected redundancy or emergency.

On the other hand, your partner may be worried that if you don't have exciting experiences together, you will both get bored with one another and the relationship will go stale.

Your partner may also tell you that they feel the need to have a once-in-a-lifetime trip, rather than go to the same old places year after year. "What do you need here?" and "What worries you about this?" are two good questions to ask when unearthing fears and needs.

---

[40] Dvorsky, G. (2016). *The Secrets To Handling Passive-Aggressive People*. gizmodo.com

As long as you are both willing to take one another's feelings into account, you will be on the right track to a solution that works for you both. Understanding one another's fears and needs is a great basis for compromise.

For example, having agreed that you both want to make good memories and relax, and having identified that your partner feels the need to take a really special trip, you could schedule an evening devoted to finding cost-effective yet "quirky" vacation ideas. You could even make a game of it, challenging one another to come up with the most interesting idea possible within an agreed budget.

Step 4 – Know what to do if you can't agree. From time to time, you'll come up against a no-win situation. This tends to happen when two people hold strong beliefs that mean a lot to them, or when their personal preferences are nonnegotiable.

For example, if you want to adopt a child but your partner only wants to have a child that is biologically their own, there is no room for compromise if you are both unwilling to budge.

In a no-win situation, your job is to resist the urge to become aggressive (and impose your will on the other person) or passive (and just agree to what the other person wants). It might sound obvious, but there doesn't have to be a "winner" and a "loser."

Acknowledging that another person has a different perspective to your own does not mean that you are agreeing with them. It means that you have the <u>emotional intelligence</u> to understand that you are both separate individuals who have the right to your own opinions.

Be willing to entertain the possibility that you will have to agree to disagree, and that both of you might have to endure some discomfort or even some emotional pain as a result.

Remember that just because someone disagrees with you, it doesn't mean that your opinions are "bad." Good people can and do hold different opinions! Emotionally mature adults know that agreement is great and compromise is good, but some situations are just dead ends.

Step 5 – Look inside yourself, and monitor your internal dialogue. When you can't reach an agreement with another person, you need to focus on what you can change – your own reactions. You cannot control what other people do or think, but you have the power to decide whether you will let their opinions change you.

Sometimes, things just won't work out, and some people won't agree with you – and that's OK. Check that you aren't holding on to any resentment. If you find yourself thinking negative thoughts like "Nothing ever goes my way," or "Life is out to get me," you need to change your mindset before you can move forward.

Don't skip this step. Our inner dialogue has the power to shape our mood, and if you do not address your negative thoughts, they will slowly color your entire outlook on life.

Research has shown that people who tend to think negative thoughts are vulnerable to depression. Furthermore, negativity keeps people stuck in a low mood. It's a vicious cycle! Accept your negative thoughts, but challenge them. Don't let them weigh you down.[41]

The quickest way to overcome these thoughts is to find at least three pieces of evidence that contradicts them. If possible, note them down on a piece of paper.

For instance, if you find yourself thinking that nothing ever goes your way, list three pieces of good luck you have experienced over the past year. A bit of gratitude can make a big difference!

Finally, you need to make a plan that accommodates your own needs as far as is reasonably possible. For example, to continue with the scenario above, you may find

---

[41] Teasdale, J.D. (1983). Negative thinking in depression: Cause, effect, or reciprocal relationship? *Advances in Behavior Research and Therapy, 5, 1,* 3-25.

that there is no way to bridge the gap between your partner's preferred option (to have a child that is biologically related to you) and your preferred option (to adopt a child).

This would undoubtedly be a hard situation, but even in the most difficult of circumstances, you do have options. In this case, you could decide that you will choose to remain childfree, to leave the relationship and find another partner whose needs are more compatible with your own, or to fulfil your need to nurture a young person by working in a child-centered career. Your options may not be ideal, but you can still use your free will and good judgment to make the best of a tough situation.

For the sake of your relationship, it's vital that you make peace with reality – accepting what is, and not dwelling on what might have been. If that means talking to a third party, such as a counselor, then so be it. Carrying around resentment and dissatisfaction will not only make you feel bad, but it will also damage your relationship.

Of course, there are some situations in which two people cannot hope to have a meaningful discussion. In the next chapter, I'm going to talk about how you can deal with toxic situations that, if left unchecked, will wreak havoc on your mental health.

Chapter 7: How to Identify & Handle Verbal Abuse

When the topic of abuse comes up, most people automatically think of physical assault. But what about abuse that doesn't involve any bodily contact? Sadly, too many of us are taught that as long as someone isn't actually causing you physical harm, they aren't an abuser. This belief can keep someone locked into an abusive relationship, because they don't realize that verbal abuse isn't normal.

Physical abuse is usually obvious – either someone is using force against you, or they are not. But when it comes to verbal abuse, the picture can be more confusing.[42] In this chapter, I'll give you a quick primer on verbal abuse, how to spot it, why it is so damaging to your relationship, and how to handle the situation.

Anyone can be on the receiving end of verbal abuse. Male, female, heterosexual, homosexual, young or old – anyone can experience it.

I'm going to focus on verbal abuse between romantic partners, but most of this chapter also applies to abusive friendships or family relationships. You don't necessarily have to end your relationship with someone who verbally abuses you.

However, for the sake of your mental health, you should at least arm yourself with the knowledge you need before making a decision.

Verbal abuse should always be taken seriously. It can cause depression, anxiety, low self-esteem, and social withdrawal.[43] You should also know that it's not unusual for verbal abuse to escalate to physical violence.[44]

So what is verbal abuse?

---

[42] Garam, J. (2016). *Are You The Victim Of Verbal Abuse Without Even Realizing It? 10 Things You Need To Know.* prevention.com
[43] Morningside Recovery. (2017). *Understanding Verbal Abuse.* morningsiderecovery.com
[44] Ibid.

When someone deliberately speaks to you in a way that causes you emotional harm, they are verbally abusing you. There are two main facets of verbal abuse. The first is what someone is saying. The second is how they are saying it.

The most obvious form of verbal abuse is name calling. In a relationship between two adults, there is no justification for this behavior. It is never constructive, and is a tactic used to intimidate or silence the other person into submission.

If someone is using derogatory language towards you, deliberately provoking you, or otherwise making you feel bad using their words or tone of voice, you are being verbally abused.

Other forms of verbally abusive behavior include the following[45]:

Belittling someone else's opinions: It's fine to disagree with someone, but putting their views down for no good reason and using unnecessarily harsh words (e.g. "That's a really stupid opinion, why on earth would anyone think that?") is abusive.

Gaslighting: This is form of abuse that attempts to change a victim's perception of reality. The aim is to confuse the victim and undermine their confidence. For example, an abuser might try to convince the victim that they forgot the abuser's birthday the previous year, even though the latter knows full well that they did not. When it works, gaslighting makes the victim feel as though they are going mad. This leaves them vulnerable to manipulation.

Blaming: Verbal abusers often shift the blame for their own behavior onto their victims. For example, if they become angry, they might tell the victim that it's their fault for making them feel bad. This tactic encourages the victim to comply with the abuser's demands in the hope that they will avoid triggering another outburst.

Excessive judgment or criticism: Abusive judgments and criticisms are not delivered with the other person's best interests at heart. Verbal abusers use harsh

---

[45] Brogaard, B. (2015). *15 Common Forms of Verbal Abuse in Relationships.* psychologytoday.com

judgments as a way of intimidating others. By confidently asserting their opinions as though they are absolute truths, they try to create a power dynamic that always lets them come out on top.

Deliberate withholding: We all need to keep our thoughts and feelings private from time to time. No one is obliged to share absolutely everything with their partner. However, verbal abusers intentionally use withholding tactics as a way of keeping their partner "on edge."

A verbal abuser may look sad or angry, but insist that nothing is wrong when confronted. They may later accuse their victim of "not caring." Withholding is therefore both abusive and passive-aggressive.

Trivializing: This involves cutting down a partner and minimizing their achievements, their social skills, or even the amount of time and effort they put into the relationship. For example, an abuser might claim that their partner gives them "no attention" or "doesn't care," even if it's obvious that this isn't the case. Trivializing can slowly chip away at someone's self-esteem.

Unfortunately, I have witnessed this form of verbal abuse in my own family. My mother's sister is now divorced, but when I was a child she was married to a man who would take every opportunity to sneer at her achievements.

For example, my aunt once managed to get a great job working at a legal firm. She had been trying to get a paralegal position for years, so it was a really big achievement.

When she told her husband the news, he stared at her for a few moments, shrugged his shoulders, and sighed.

"That office will be full of young people just starting out in their careers," he said. "Won't that make you feel a bit old?" He didn't offer her any congratulations whatsoever.

My aunt still took the job, but my mother reported that she felt self-conscious about her age for weeks after his nasty remarks. Never underestimate the power of words.

Denial: Abusers have a habit of forgetting what they have said and done. Some will deny that they have ever abused their partner. This is a form of gaslighting. Denial leaves the victim feeling disoriented and questioning their own reality, which makes it harder to take an objective look at the situation.

On the other hand, some abusers will be full of remorse and fake apologies. They will tell their victim how sorry they are, and promise that it will never happen again. But guess what? The cycle usually starts over.

Whether it spans a few days or several months, it will repeat itself time and time again until someone deliberately breaks the pattern. This behavior is so common that it is known as the "cycle of abuse."

What do all these forms of abuse have in common? In short, every single one allows the perpetrator to dominate the victim by wearing them down. Whether they openly admit it or not, an abuser's goal is to control their victim by undermining their confidence.

There are several theories that try to account for why someone might become verbally abusive. Some abusers find it hard to regulate their own emotions, and they can't handle negative feelings. As a result, they lash out at others.

Experiences of childhood abuse also seem to lay the groundwork for inappropriate behavior later in life. Specifically, if an individual is left traumatized by abuse they witnessed or experienced in childhood, they are more likely to use abusive tactics in their adult relationships.[46]

---

[46] Askin, C. (2015). *Five Reasons People Abuse Their Partners.* psychologytoday.com

I'll let the experts work out the ultimate answer! For the purposes of this chapter, I'm more concerned with providing practical strategies that will help you handle verbal abuse.

Strategies for handling verbal abuse

Record conversations: Keep a recording device discreetly tucked away in the living room (or wherever the verbal abuse tends to occur), or use your phone to record conversations with your partner. This will keep you sane, because listening to prior conversations will help you spot patterns of abuse. It is a reality check.

Furthermore, if your partner tends to deny their abuse or accuses you of saying things that never passed your lips, these records will help you keep track of who really said what to whom. Recordings are also useful evidence that can be used in therapy, or even in court cases.

Keep a diary of key events: Along with recordings, keep a log of the abuse. Note down dates, times, and circumstances. Recordings are useful, but they don't always capture the events that precede abuse. Keep your diary hidden, or use a password protected file on your phone or computer.

Practice changing your inner dialogue: Verbal abuse is particularly distressing if the victim believes what the perpetrator is saying about them. As I've mentioned earlier in this book, you can't control other people, but you can control your own reactions. If you can learn how to tell yourself that an abuser is telling you lies so that they can try to control you, their words will carry less weight.

Rather than reacting to what they are saying as though it were true, use your inner dialogue as a defense mechanism.

For example, if someone tells you that you are ugly, make a conscious effort to tell yourself that they spouting garbage because they don't want to treat you as an equal. This won't stop the abuse, but it is a short-term measure that can help protect your self-esteem.

If it's safe to do so, defend your boundaries: Sometimes, asserting your boundaries will only aggravate a verbal abuser, or even trigger physical violence. However, if possible, tell them that you won't tolerate their behavior.

Refer back to the chapter on setting and upholding boundaries for more advice on how to do this. Do not try to reason with a verbal abuser. They are not interested in having a constructive conversation – they want to assert their power.

Get a reality check from someone you trust: Confide in a trusted friend or relative, and ask them to serve as a reality check. Someone who is on the outside looking in at your relationship is in a better place to tell you whether your experiences are normal.

Be warned – not everyone understands what verbal abuse is, and some will trivialize your experience. If they say things like "But it's not that bad," "Everyone has fights," and "But he or she is a good person underneath," find someone else to support you.

Create an identity that doesn't depend on anyone else's validation: The more secure you are in yourself, the less likely you are to be hurt by your partner's cruel words. Channel your energy into building friendships, strengthening family bonds, and expanding your social and professional networks.

Seek therapy: In an ideal world, a verbal abuser would take themselves to therapy and admit that they need help. Unfortunately, this rarely happens, because they believe that their behavior is totally reasonable.[47]

However, this doesn't mean that the victim can't benefit from therapy. If your relationship is making you unhappy, a therapist with experience in abuse can help you make sense of the situation. If you can convince your partner to enter couples therapy, then your relationship might stand a chance.

---

[47] Bancroft, L. (2003). *Why Does He Do That? Inside the Minds of Angry and Controlling Men.* New York, NY: Berkly.

Never respond with abuse of your own: Under threat, you might want to defend yourself by returning someone's insults and aggression. This is a terrible strategy, and one to be avoided at all costs. Abusing someone else, even if you are acting in self-defense, means acting against your morals and values.

It also gives your abuser ammunition to use against you in the future. Whenever you try to set a boundary or let them know that you are unhappy with their behavior, they'll point out that you aren't so perfect yourself.

Why a victim can find it hard to leave an abuser

Those who have never experienced an abusive relationship tend to wonder why the victim doesn't just leave. Unfortunately, it isn't quite so simple. Some victims are dependent on their abusers for money, housing, or other forms of support.

Others enter a state of denial, clinging onto hope that the other person will eventually see the light and change their ways, even though this is unlikely to happen unless they enter therapy and admit that they need to do some serious work on themselves.[48]

Lots of abusers treat their victims well in the early stages of the relationship – just long enough for the victim to fall in love. By the time the abuse begins, the victim will find it hard to end the relationship. Over time, they start to see the abuse as normal, and forget what it was like to live a life free from emotional turmoil.

If they had low self-esteem before entering the relationship, they may come to believe that they somehow deserve the abuse. Finally, because abuse often comes in cycles, a victim might hope that the "nice" phase will last forever. It can take years before they face reality and acknowledge that nothing will change without drastic intervention.

---

[48] Ibid.

If you need to talk to someone about your relationship, or get help to break free from an abuser, there are several services that can help you decide how to move forward. The National Domestic Violence Hotline (thehotline.org) offers a telephone and online service that provides support 365 days a year. If you are a woman, the government's Women's Health website (womenshealth.gov) is a good starting point.

Obviously, an abusive person is a negative influence. However, not all negative people are abusive. In the next chapter, I'll show you how to handle everyday negativity.

Chapter 8: Dealing with Negative People

In the previous chapter, we looked at verbal abuse. But what about those people who aren't abusive, but still manage to drag your mood down? In this section, I'll tell you how to spot a negative person – they aren't quite as obvious as you might think – and how to stay positive even if you have to deal with them on a regular basis.

Not all negative people are the same!

So, what do I mean by "negative people"? Here's a quick rundown of the most common types:

Straight-up negative individuals

These are easy to spot. They are the people who never have anything good to say about anyone or anything. They seem to suck the life out of a room. Other people tend to avoid them whenever possible.

Martyrs

You might not recognize a Martyr at first. They present themselves as someone who always puts the needs of others before their own. Sounds good, right?

Unfortunately, they then complain that they have no time for themselves, that no one appreciates them, and so on. After a while, this gets very wearing. Don't be fooled – a Martyr actually enjoys wearing themselves out, because it gives them a reason to complain.

People who relentlessly judge everyone

I admit it – we all judge others. Everyone has an opinion, and that's OK. However, judgmental people never hold back. If someone isn't perfect, they'll let you know. Actually, they'll let you know over and over again.

Over time, you'll get the feeling that they will start judging you behind your back. (Too late – I can almost guarantee they've already started.)

People who distract you from your goals

Distractors don't necessarily *sound* negative, which can make them hard to spot. It's what they do, rather than what they say, that should sound your alarm bells. Basically, a Distractor takes up a lot of your time and energy to the extent that your goals start to suffer.[49]

Distractors can make you feel suffocated and even a little helpless, because you aren't sure how to get rid of them! A Distractor will typically talk to you for hours about nothing of real importance, use you as a sounding board, or subtly recruit you to carry out tasks for them.

The two-step plan for dealing with negative people

I'll give it to you straight: The best way to deal with a negative person is to stop interacting with them. I don't care whether you feel sorry for them or want to help in some way – they are still bad news.

Why? Because, even if you are fascinated by psychology and the science of human behavior, you aren't here to play the role of therapist to negative people. You could spend hours trying to analyze their behavior, and it won't get you anywhere.

In fact, you probably know some people who waste their precious time trying to "figure out" their troublesome relatives, friends, or colleagues – to no avail. Do not fall into this trap!

OK, I know what you're thinking. You can cut out negative acquaintances, avoid colleagues from other departments at work, and reduce the time you spend with

---

[49] Hankel, I. (2016). *Stay Away From These 5 Types Of Negative People*. youtube.com

distant family members, but what about those people you really can't avoid? I personally use a two-pronged strategy with these individuals.

First, I make sure my mindset is in the right place. Second, I have an arsenal of communication strategies that shut down their negativity so that I can carry on living my life in peace.

Step One: Change your attitude

If you can't change someone else, don't despair. You can always change how you react to a situation.

Think back to your last interaction with a negative person. I'm going to use an example that happened to me a few months ago with my neighbor. I was heading out the door to work one morning, and she was putting out birdseed in her yard. I'll call her "Sally:"

ME: "Hi Sally! Isn't the weather great?"

SALLY: "It's not usually this hot in March. No rain for weeks!"

ME: "It is pretty warm for the time of year, true."

SALLY: "That's probably why the grass looks awful. Anyway, you're out the door early this morning."

ME: "Yes, I've got a meeting with a new client, I'm excited to work with them!"

SALLY: "You work a lot, don't you? I don't get why people are so driven to work all the time these days. I bet you're exhausted by the end of the week."

At this point, I wrapped the conversation up with a cheery farewell and hopped into my car. It definitely wasn't my ideal start to the morning! Does this story resonate with you? Most of us have met people like this!

I can't cut Sally out of my life completely. I typically see her a couple of times per day, and I want to maintain a cordial relationship with all my neighbors. Luckily, I don't have to let her bad moods drag me down. Here are the tools I use in this kind of situation.

Shifting your mindset

Look at the following phrases. Can you spot the subtle difference?

"Sally is a negative person."

"Sally has a lot of negativity."

In the first sentence, we're assuming that Sally is, at heart, a negative person. If you've spent time around someone and they have always behaved in a negative manner, this is a fair assessment. After all, we can only draw conclusions based on what we have experienced.

However, I find the second sentence more interesting. Although it isn't the most elegant phrase I have ever written, it is very useful when it comes to staying positive in the face of someone else's complaints, griping, and whining.

The key word here is "has." Sally owns her negativity. It is hers alone. It isn't mine, it isn't her husband's, it doesn't belong to anyone else. I don't have to accept it.

When I realized that I can let someone own their attitude, and I can make my own decision as to whether I want to engage with it or ignore it, negative people started to bother me less and less.

Remember:

1. Just as other people have no right to control your mood, you don't have the right to control theirs.

2. When you encounter negativity, you don't have to take it on board.

3. You are not obliged to lower yourself to anyone else's level. You are not responsible for easing anyone's suffering, or cheering them up.[50]

4. It isn't healthy to allow your feelings to be dictated by someone else's moods. In fact, it's a sign of codependency. As you know, codependency doesn't make for healthy relationships.

5. Anyone who assumes that your role in a relationship is to listen to their complaints for hours, or to cheer them up, is bad news. They will drain your energy – fast.

Using Hanlon's Razor to deal with judgmental people

How many times have you heard someone voice a really stupid, toxic opinion that's left you in a bad mood for the rest of the day? I have! Fortunately, I came across a great quote that transformed the way I dealt with judgmental people.

You've probably heard of Occam's Razor: The notion that the simplest solution is usually most likely to be correct. But what about Hanlon's Razor? Attributed to the author Robert J. Hanlon, it goes like this:

"Never attribute to malice that which can be adequately explained by stupidity.[51]*"*

Hanlon's Razor is a useful reminder that most of the negative, judgmental people I come across aren't waging a personal campaign against me. Instead, they are probably making stupid, ill-informed remarks because they are actually - wait for it - ill-formed, stupid, or both. I can't really hold that against them. In most cases, they probably know no better.

---

[50] Power Of Positivity. (2017). *9 Positive Ways to Deal With Negative People*. powerofpositivity.com
[51] Sturm, M. (2017). *Hanlon's Razor: How to Avoid Common Missteps in Judgment*. medium.com

And if they do? Well, I don't have the time to prove it, and choosing to believe that they are just stupid rather than malicious helps me stay calm. If someone wants to debate a particular point with me, I'll happily have a constructive discussion, but for the most part I make a point of brushing off ignorant comments.

You can even turn it into a game! Every time I encounter a negative, judgmental person speak, I think "Hanlon! Hanlon!" It makes me smile, and helps me see past their silly remarks.

When it comes to dealing with Sally, I remind myself that because she has never held down a regular job (she is a homemaker, and her husband is the breadwinner), it's unlikely that she has a clue what she's talking about when it comes to careers and time management in the workplace.

Step Two: Use these three phrases that will shut down negativity

There are no magic words that will work on every negative person. The right approach will depend on your relationship, the amount of time you have available, and the cause of their problem.

Of course, if you are in a romantic relationship with the other person, you will be more inclined to take a more understanding approach – but this doesn't mean that you have to listen to their negativity for hours on end.

Here are three useful phrases to use with someone who is whining just for the hell of it:

"That's unfortunate. Did anything positive come out of it?:" Negative people are taken aback by this tactic. It forces them either to acknowledge that the situation isn't 100% bad, or it forces them to say "No, nothing!" which provides you with a great opportunity to say "That sucks!" and change the subject.[52]

---

[52] Frost, A. (2017). *7 Perfect Replies to (Politely) Shut Down Negative People.* themuse.com

"I hear what you're saying, but talking like this isn't going to change the situation. I'm going to suggest that we talk about something else:" This allows the other person to feel heard, but firmly steers the conversation in a more positive direction.

"What do you need me to do?:" This is a less aggressive alternative to "Well, what can I do about it?," but it accomplishes the same objective. It forces the other person to stop venting and engage with the real issue – can a problem be fixed and, if so, how?

The complainer will have to admit that there is nothing you can do (which will highlight how pointless it is for them to keep venting) or, if you can help in some way, the conversation can then focus on constructive problem-solving.

Dealing with negative prophets

Resist the urge to argue with those who make negative predictions for the sake of it. They aren't looking for a proper debate on the matter at hand.

If they were, they would have outlined the reasons for their position and asked for your feedback. When someone prophesizes doom just because they feel the need to be a downer, be smart and shut it down.

Depending on the relationship you have with this person, and how sensitive they are to rejection, you could try some of these lines.

Notice that they are diversionary tactics. This is because ignoring the other person will make you appear rude, but engaging with them will just suck you down into their black hole.

"We'll wait and see. Anyway..."

"Thank you for your input. So anyway..."

"I'll bear that in mind. In the meantime..."

"It's always good to have another perspective. Now, let's move on to..."

"It's funny how two people can see the same situation so differently! So, as I was saying..."

"True, I guess that might happen! So I'm sure we'd all rather talk about something more positive...."

Stick to your boundaries

By now, you'll know that I'm keen on boundaries as a tool in relationships. They come in handy when you have to deal with negative people.

Think of their negativity as a behavior that you don't have to tolerate. If someone was insulting you, or invading your personal space, you would assert your boundaries until they started to behave like a reasonable human being. When confronted by someone's negativity, you can use the same principles.

Let's look at how this might work in practice. I didn't have to use my imagination to come up with this example – it actually happened to me at a family gathering a few weeks ago. I was sat next to my cousin at the dinner table.

COUSIN: *My daughter hasn't decided on her college major yet.*

ME: *It can be hard to know what you want to do at her age.*

COUSIN: *She's trying to decide between Communications and Psychology. What a waste of time.*

ME: *What do you mean by "a waste of time?"*

COUSIN: *They're both useless. What kind of career is she going to get?*

ME: In my experience, anyone can make a great career for themselves if they make a good plan and stick to it. Lots of people end up in careers that aren't related to their college major.

[At this point, I sensed that my cousin wasn't really trying to have a conversation. All he wanted to do was complain about his daughter's choices. Because he knows that I have an interest in psychology, I suspected he was also trying to goad me. I decided to gently call him out on his negativity, and defend my boundaries.]

COUSIN: Yeah, well you would say that. You know what? I think she should think about nursing. Something that will help people.

ME: You seem really down on psychology. That's your opinion, which is fine, but doesn't make me feel good to hear you talk like that when you know it's what I do for a living. Please can we change the subject? Otherwise I'm going to have to ignore you and talk to my dessert instead!

[A touch of humor can work well to diffuse a situation.]

COUSIN: Well....OK. I guess. Have you picked out that new car yet?

Was the conversation slightly awkward? Yes. Did I have to think carefully before asserting my boundary? Yes. But did it work out in the end? Definitely! What's more, I'm willing to bet that my cousin will think twice in the future before subjecting me to his pointless negativity.

Model positive behavior

A long-term approach to conquering negativity is positive role modeling. Earlier in this chapter, I emphasized that you are not responsible for someone else's behavior, only your responses.

On the other hand, if you can make yourself happier and encourage someone else to be more positive, that's got to be a win-win situation!

Modeling positive behavior lets you do precisely that. You don't need to be excessively cheerful, but if you can do the following on a consistent basis, the negative people around you might follow suit:

1. Take a realistic view of every situation, but emphasize the positive.

2. Be clear what you will and won't accept from other people.

3. Defend your boundaries.

4. Take responsibility for your own emotions.

5. Apologize when you have offended someone, and offer to make amends where appropriate.

6. Choose positive people as partners, friends, and acquaintances.

What about those who are so stuck in their ways that they cling onto their negativity like a life raft?

There's another advantage to using the modeling technique. Cynical, passive-aggressive people might roll their eyes at your positivity, but the great news is that they will start to leave you alone!

Happiness and optimism make these people uncomfortable, so they are effective repellants.

Chapter 9: Identifying & Handling Love Addiction

It's normal to want a romantic relationship, but some people become completely obsessed with love and romance. Love addiction can destroy lives, and it can prevent the addict forming healthy relationships.

The term "love addict" is casually thrown around in the media and in self-help circles, but what does it really mean? Here are the main symptoms[53]:

A general obsession with "romance:" Did you often daydream about your future husband or wife as a kid? Have you always gone for romantic music, books, and movies? Do you always want to know what's going on in your friends' love lives?

The belief that falling in love is the solution to all your problems: When you are having a bad day, do you slip into a fantasy that ends with someone rescuing you from all life's issues, both trivial and serious? Is your idea of heaven a never-ending vacation with someone who absolutely adores you?

A habit of treating every social occasion as a chance to find a love interest: Love addicts are constantly watching out for someone who makes them feel special and adored. If you start scanning the room for potential mates at every party (or even at every business meeting!) then you may well have a problem.

A tendency to jump from one intense relationship to another: Do you tend to have short-lived, intense relationships that fizzle out quickly? Do you try to forge a "deep" connection with someone within days (or even hours) of meeting them, and feel positively euphoric if they seem to return your feelings?

A tendency to go for potential rather than reality: When you meet someone, do you start thinking how you could improve them? When you can't accept your partner for who they are, you're probably looking for someone you can shape to fit your image of a "good partner," rather than someone real to love.[54]

---

[53] Smith, A. (2010). *How To Break the Pattern of Love Addiction.* psychologytoday.com
[54] Lue, N. (2013). *The Dreamer and the Fantasy Relationship.* London, England: CreateSpace.

A fear of being single: This one is self-explanatory. If you feel lonely at the mere thought of being single, this is a big warning sign. A series of short, overlapping relationships is common in love addiction.

An inability to boost your own self-esteem: Love addicts look to their partners to affirm their self-worth. If you feel empty without someone in your life, and find it hard to imagine who you are when you are not part of a couple, this implies that you are hooked on the idea of having someone to validate you.

A reputation as a love addict or serial dater in your social circle: Do the people who know you best ever make jokes about your chaotic love life? Maybe they have even used the words "love addict" to describe you. As the saying goes, "Many a true word is spoken in jest."

There's nothing wrong with falling head over heels in the early stages of a relationship. The trouble starts when we see love as not merely a fantastic experience in our lives, but as the only important experience worth having.

When your happiness hinges on someone else reciprocating your love, you are taking a huge risk. If they don't return your feelings, you will be left heartbroken. To distract yourself from the pain, you might jump into another intense relationship...and the cycle will continue.[55]

The horrible irony is that these behaviors actually repel anyone who is worth having as a partner. No sane individual is going to want to date a love addict. They might not be familiar with the term, but they will run when they realize what they are dealing with.

After all, who wants to invite so much drama into their life? Only other drama queens (or kings), and they are more trouble than they're worth. If you truly want a real relationship, you need to take love addiction seriously.

---

[55] John, C. (2016). *I Love You But: The "Dance" Of Love Addiction.* intervene.org.uk

Note that not all love addicts have crushes on people they know. Some people become obsessed with famous people they will never meet. In extreme cases, love addicts may become fixated on a fictional character!

I also want to make it clear that both men and women can develop love addiction. It's more socially acceptable for women to talk about their feelings, but I promise you that there are men facing similar problems.

Much has been written on why some people get hooked on love. This isn't a therapy manual, so I'm not going to write an essay on all the possible causes.

However, I think it's important to make one point. The typical love addict feels the need to "prove themselves" to someone who isn't interested in returning their feelings.

A love addict has typically felt insecure and unloved from a young age. Psychologists have observed that love addicts regularly go for narcissists and emotionally unavailable people, because it gives them the chance to prove themselves by winning the affection of someone who doesn't seem willing to give it.

After all, love addiction isn't really about love – it's about using drama and excitement to fill a void, and to get the approval the addict was not shown in childhood.[56]

How to overcome love addiction

Recovery from love addiction requires two things. First, you have to build for yourself an identity that does not revolve around catching and keeping a partner.

This involves examining your relationship history, growing your own interests, nurturing a supportive social circle, and pursuing goals and dreams that have nothing to do with love and romance.

---

[56] Ibid.

You might need to see a therapist, attend support groups, or read books by love addiction experts. I recommend *Addiction to Love* by Susan Peabody, which sets out exactly where love addiction comes from, and the main steps you must take if you want to change.

Second, you need to change how you relate to other people. You can't have an authentic relationship if you cast someone in the role of your next great love. The only way to establish a real connection is to take off your rose-tinted glasses and take your time in building a relationship.

Communication skills for love addicts

Learn how to talk about everyday issues: We tend to talk about what we value most. If you are a love addict, your primary focus of conversation will be your relationships, your crushes, your partners, or your ex-partners.

I hate to break it to you, but your family and friends probably got sick of it years ago. Love addiction tends to damage relationships in two ways.

First, the object of your obsession (your love interest) takes your attention away from family and friends. Second, talking about the same topic over and over again (such as your love interest or your latest relationship drama) will not endear you to anyone.

It's time to change the script. If you don't have any hobbies or interests to talk about, get some. Alternatively, just keep the conversation focused on the other person.

Hold back on the most intimate details of your life!: Healthy relationships are based on a gradual disclosure of information. Love addicts spill their guts within days, or even hours, of meeting someone new. They do this in the hope that it will create an immediate sense of intimacy. They tell potential love interests every little detail, thinking that they will earn their pity, compassion, and care.

This doesn't work. Normal, healthy people are turned off when someone tells them everything about their problems, their personal life, and their romantic fantasies.[57]

Learn how to make small talk, how to ask someone suitable questions that will let you develop healthy rapport, and how to move a relationship along at a reasonable pace.

Talk to people that will never interest you romantically: Recovery from love addiction involves building positive relationships with people who will only be friends, never romantic partners.

Where can you meet new friends? Everywhere! Seek them out at work, via your existing friends, at adult education classes, and special interest groups.

Set yourself the challenge of making two new friends that you will never find physically or romantically attractive. Ideally, these friends should be in stable, happy relationships that you can use as models in the future.

Don't be surprised if you find it hard to feel interested in platonic relationships. It will take time to shake your assumption that if someone can't provide you with romantic validation then they aren't worth talking to.

Drop the excessive texts and emails and communicate face to face: There's nothing like a text, instant message, or social media post to fire up your imagination.

Everyone falls into the trap of reading too much into written messages from time to time. For example, who hasn't pondered whether "Xxx" at the end of a text means something significant?

Keep it real. Spend time face to face rather than swapping endless online messages. This is good advice for anyone, but it is particularly important for love addicts, who have a tendency to over-analyze every little message from a potential love interest.

---

[57] Lue, N. (2011). *Mr Unavailable & The Fallback Girl: The Definitive Guide To Understanding Emotionally Unavailable Men And The Women That Love Them*. London, England: Natalie Lue Publishing.

Know when it's time to sever all ties: If you are a love addict, you need to learn how to cut contact with someone who is triggering your obsessive thoughts and behaviors.

Hundreds of articles have been written on this concept, known as the "No Contact Rule," but it comes down to this – as soon as you realize that someone is only a fantasy figure or distraction, stop engaging with them.

Tell them that the interactions aren't working for you, and that you no longer wish to continue the "relationship."[58] No calls, no emails, no texting, no dates, no hookups.

If you have to work or parent with this person, keep your interactions short and civil. Stop fueling the on-off, on-off cycle that so many love addicts fall into! I know that this is far from easy. In fact, it can be a brutal process.

Have a support system in place. Confide in close platonic friends. Start going to a therapist. Join a well-moderated online forum. Just make sure you have an outlet for the tough emotions you will face.

Get real with yourself about someone else's intentions: If you tend to kid yourself that someone is interested in you just because it fits the fantasy inside your head, it's time to pay attention to what they are actually doing, not what they are saying.

Anyone can sit down and fire off a few flirtatious text messages, but it takes effort to show up for proper dates, to set aside half an hour for a meaningful phone call, and so on.

If you are a love addict, you need to realize that the majority of romantic relationships fail, and it's pointless to try and make one work at the cost of your sanity.

---

[58] Robarge, A. (2017). *End Love Addiction by Burning the Bridge: On Again Off Again Relationships.* youtube.com

Think about it. How many people marry their first love? Very few. It is normal to date at least a few people before settling down.

Accepting the reality of dating will make you more secure in your love life, as you will know that a failed relationship does not mean that you are "unlovable" or inadequate in any way.

What if you find yourself dating a love addict?

To be brutally honest, I wouldn't recommend that you carry on seeing someone if you learn that they are a love addict. If they come out and tell you that they "suffer from love addiction," it's a huge red flag.

Unless they are in the process of getting help, whether that entails going to a therapist or a peer support group such as Sex and Love Addicts Anonymous, their issues will probably kill your relationship.

Your partner will have trouble seeing you and the relationship in a realistic light, and they will need endless reassurance. They will always be seeking that romantic "high," and getting upset when their romantic partner (i.e. you) doesn't meet their expectations.

Earlier in this chapter, I mentioned that no sane, healthy person would want to date a love addict. If you realize that the person you are dating is showing signs of love addiction, you need to take a look at your own role in the dynamic.

Love addicts are attracted to people who aren't emotionally available – those who tend to toss out crumbs of affection, who aren't really able to make a commitment, and have an erratic communication style.

This is why it's so important to make sure that you are in the right mindset before you start dating. If you aren't sure what you want, or even whether you want to be in a relationship at all, you are more likely to attract the attention of people who are desperate to earn the approval of someone who isn't sure whether they want to give it.

Take a few steps back. Are you sure that you want to make yourself emotionally vulnerable? Do you really want to open up to another person? If not, you aren't in a position to date right now.

I want to end on a positive note. Yes, love addiction is painful, and it is hard to overcome. On the other hand, if you have to deal with a love addiction, you have a golden opportunity to examine your beliefs about relationships and rebuild great communication skills from the ground up.

Your problems can become a springboard for self-development that will set you up for healthy bonds in every area of your life.

Part II – Developing the Communication Skills You Need for Great Relationships

Chapter 10: Understanding Different Communication Styles

Have you ever tried to have a conversation with someone, only to feel as though the two of you are speaking different languages?

Perhaps you've met someone who, on paper, seems to be just the kind of person you'd want as a partner or friend, but never quite seems to "get" you? Don't give up yet! This situation is pretty common and there is a simple explanation.

In this chapter, I'll explain why we all communicate in slightly different ways, and how to forge a connection with anyone, regardless of their communication style.

Lots of us want to understand how and why we sometimes find it hard to get along with others. I'm going to introduce a theory that has been used by leading global businesses, including Coca-Cola and Apple, and by the NASA recruitment team! If it's good enough for NASA, it's good enough for me.

The link between personality and communication style

Back in the 1970s, psychologist Taibi Kahler started researching the link between an individual's personality type and their communication style. He started his career as a psychologist interested in psychotherapy.

Specifically, he wondered what kinds of negative thought patterns caused mental health problems such as depression. He was also interested in the question of whether it was possible to predict how someone would respond to therapy based on their personality and way of speaking.[59]

He reasoned that if he could understand how someone was likely to behave whilst under stress, and the style of communication they preferred to use when talking to other people, it would be easier to connect with them in psychotherapy.

---

[59] Kahler, T. (n.d.) *The Process Model.* pcmoceania.com

The beauty of this theory is that it isn't just useful for therapists. Anyone who wants to understand why people misunderstand one another can benefit.

If you and your partner, friend or colleague just can't seem to appreciate what the other is saying, it might be down to a clash in communication styles.

Of course, it's perfectly possible to communicate with any personality type using the skills in this book. However, I've found this model to be an excellent tool when it comes to understanding others.

Once you've figured out someone's primary personality type and method of communication, you'll find that your relationships will become smoother.

The six key personality types

Kahler figured out that most people fall into one of the following categories. No one is locked into these patterns forever. We all contain elements of these six personalities, and each style has its own motivations and communication styles.[60] However, we all tend to gravitate towards one of these "types:"

Harmonizers

[30% of Americans fit this category, and 75% of Harmonizers are women]

Here's how you can spot a Harmonizer:

1. They are gentle, compassionate, and like to nurture others
2. They are sensitive and easily hurt
3. They like to build bonds by exchanging personal stories
4. They are great at validating other people
5. They don't like to be alone, and they love helping others

---

[60] Regier, N. (2015). *This is how NASA used to hire its astronauts 20 years ago – and it still works today.* qz.com

6. They enjoy the visual arts, good food, and uplifting music – their senses are highly attuned to stimuli
7. When they are upset, they tend to become less assertive, experience a loss of confidence, and they become flustered

How should you talk to a Harmonizer?

1. They love affirmations such as "You're so generous" and "You're such a good listener," so use them wherever possible
2. They like to exchange stories – a Harmonizer will appreciate it when you open up to them
3. Tell them exactly how they can help, and how much their help means to you
4. Keep tension to a minimum, never raise your voice, and stay calm in heated situations
5. Show your gentler side, as this will make them feel safe
6. Watch for signs of uncertainty, and give them plenty of praise to shore up their confidence

Thinkers

[25% of Americans fit this category, and 75% of Thinkers are male]

If you meet a Thinker, you'll notice that they:

1. Like to know precisely what is going on, and when
2. Prize logical thinking above all else
3. Deal in facts and figures
4. Value equality – if they are fighting with someone, they believe it is only right that everyone is heard
5. Prefer solitude and small groups to larger gatherings
6. Become critical of others when under stress, and can become pedantic with regards to dates, times, and schedules

How should you communicate with a Thinker?

1. Don't waffle – Thinkers like to get the facts upfront
2. If you want to win their respect, always back up your arguments with objective facts and figures
3. Praise them for their hard work rather than their personality and people skills
4. Speak to them one-on-one if possible
5. If they have upset you, relate the facts and list your feelings (bullet points work well here!)
6. Tap into their strengths by asking them for help with planning or research tasks
7. Anticipate pedantic behavior, and be ready to steer the conversation back to the original problem if necessary

Persisters

[10% of Americans fit this category, and 75% of Persisters are male]

How do you know when you've found a Persister?

1. You'll notice that they are a keen observer of people
2. They tend to hone in on the important facts of a situation quickly
3. They voice their opinions, and they hold fast to their values
4. They are conscientious, and hate leaving a job unfinished
5. They are usually introverted
6. They can be too pushy when it comes to their belief system, especially under stress
7. They expect a lot of themselves – and, sometimes, they expect too much of others

How should you communicate with a Persister?

1. Always make it clear that you respect their cherished beliefs, even if you don't agree with them
2. Praise them for all the tasks they have completed
3. Talk through problems in terms of beliefs and values – Persisters place a lot of emphasis on personal convictions
4. If you are debating or fighting with a Persister, tell them that your primary desire is to understand their beliefs
5. Be prepared to defend your boundaries if a Persister is in a dogmatic mood, because they might try to push their beliefs on you
6. Talk to them alone or in a small group – they do not like big parties!

Imaginers

[10% of Americans fit this category, and 60% of Imaginers are female]

Here's how you know you've found an Imaginer:

1. They are calm and collected, but waste no time in telling you exactly what they think
2. They are creative, and will put forward many potential solutions to a problem
3. They are highly introverted, and prefer to be alone than with others
4. When they experience a problem, they have a tendency to suffer from "paralysis by analysis"
5. They find it hard to reach out for help

Some tips for communicating with an Imaginer:

1. Respect the fact that they need a lot of time alone, and may need time to think through a situation in solitude
2. Be prepared to offer them help a few times before they will accept it
3. Outline a situation in concise terms, and ask them for help in explicit terms if you need a solution

4. Praise them for their ability to think through a problem and come up with a new perspective

Rebels

[20% of Americans fit this category, and 60% of Rebels are female]

A typical Rebel:

1. Has a high level of energy, and is fun to be around
2. Can be very creative
3. Enjoys spending time with groups of people
4. Is competitive and likes to be "the best"
5. Is quick to judge others when things go wrong, and does not like to admit personal faults
6. Is usually upbeat, but can spiral into negativity when something does not go their way

When communicating with a Rebel:

1. Match your energy to theirs – a Rebel will find you more likeable if you are enthusiastic
2. Show that you appreciate their sense of humor, and turn problem solving into a game if possible
3. Praise their imagination and efforts
4. Give them a choice between two or more options if possible – they like to express a preference
5. Be prepared for them to blame you if you have to break some bad news
6. Defend your boundaries against their negativity

Promoters

[5% of Americans fit this category, and 60% of Promoters are male]

Here's how to spot a Promoter:

1. They always want to know what is going to happen next, and when
2. They value action over thought, and they like to win
3. They are great at persuading others
4. They like spending time in groups
5. They can use their charm to manipulate other people
6. They can become bored easily, and tend to abandon half-finished projects

When communicating with a Promoter:

1. Keep the conversation focused on realities, not dreams
2. Allow them to show off their knowledge and skills
3. Let them charm and flatter you – within reasonable limits!
4. Guard yourself against manipulation by keeping your boundaries intact
5. If you sense that they are becoming bored, get what you need from them (whether that's information or a commitment to finishing a project) as soon as possible

So how can this model help you?

As you can see, each personality style comes with its own way of viewing the world. As you read through the descriptions, you probably slotted people you know into these categories.

Now think about what might happen when two people with different personalities have to work or live together. It can get messy. But when you know what you're up against, you can start thinking of strategies.

The Persister and the Promotor

I'll give you an example that shows how this theory can help us deal with others. I'm a Persister – I like to stick to my beliefs, I'm observant, and I like to see a project through to completion. A couple of years ago, I went on a few dates with a Promoter.

At the time, I was learning about personality theories and so it was a good opportunity to see how this model worked in real life!

My date was lively, charming, and a good planner when it came to setting up activities – all common Promoter traits that fit well with my personality. As you know from the descriptions above, Promoters can also become manipulative when they don't get what they want.

During our second date, she told me a story about a time she had persuaded a colleague to go against their manager's orders. As a result of her manipulation, the colleague lost his job. That put me on high alert. Normally I would have ended the relationship there and then, but I was interested to see how the situation would play out.

One night, she phoned me just to ask about my day. At least, that's what she said she was doing. Then, after a few minutes, the conversation went like this:

HER: I'm glad work went well for you. My day wasn't great.

ME: Oh no, what happened?

HER: Nothing really.

ME: OK.

[At this point, I began to think that our interaction was taking a strange turn.]

HER: Actually, I'll tell you. [Deep breath, loud swallow.] You know my cat, Monty? I had to take him to the vet today. He's really sick. He needs surgery this week. The vet says he'll die without it!

ME: That's terrible. Aw, poor Monty. It's so hard to watch an animal suffer. When's his surgery?

HER: That's the problem. It's going to cost six hundred dollars. I don't have insurance. The vet says I can pay in instalments, but the interest is really high. I don't suppose...no, I won't ask.
ME: Ask what?

HER: Could you lend me half of it?

[I had only known this woman three weeks, and I was not going to lend her any money. I stood my ground and told her that she would have to find the money elsewhere.]

HER: Typical. You don't care about anyone but yourself. I've been so nice to you. Actually, I've been thinking, you're kind of selfish. I don't know whether I want to see you again.

ME: That's a shame. I think this conversation is over.

The good news is that I had seen this behavior coming – she was a Promoter who had already told me that she had a history of manipulating people.

Obviously, I didn't know that it would take the form of a request for $300, but I wasn't exactly shocked when she tried to emotionally blackmail me. Here's the kicker – she'd never mentioned Monty before. I'm not convinced he ever existed.

I'm not saying that Promoters are "bad," just that an awareness of the different personality types, combined with your own observations, can give you an advantage over toxic people.

Using the model to solve arguments

This works best when you are both familiar with this model, and have talked about it beforehand. Let's say that you are an Imaginer, and your partner is a Rebel. As an Imaginer, you appreciate the opportunity to spend time alone to ponder a situation rather than hammer out a resolution with your partner.

Meanwhile, your Rebel would rather take a direct approach that allows you to come up with creative solutions together.

However, if you both acknowledge the differences in your communication styles, you can work on a compromise. For example, you could both take some time alone to collect your thoughts, before sitting down and making a list of all the solutions the two of you can possibly come up with in under 10 minutes.

This approach would satisfy an Imaginer's need for alone time when under stress, together with the Rebel's desire for collaboration and creativity.

Why not use this chapter as a basis for a discussion with your partner about communication styles? It could be the start of a more productive, cohesive period in your relationship.

Chapter 11: How to Validate Another Person (And Yourself!)

Aside from a sense of security and trust, what do people want most in their relationships? I can sum it up in one word: Validation. As social animals, we want to feel that people accept us for who we are.

This is especially important in romantic relationships, because they are usually the most intimate bonds we form. If our partner doesn't seem to appreciate our perspective, or support us when things get tough, we are liable to feel hurt.

Validation is a great way to let your partner know that you are always there for them. Best of all, it's easy to do once you understand the principles behind it!

What is validation?

Have you ever gone away from a conversation about a difficult or complex topic feeling as though the other person truly understood you?

Isn't it wonderful when someone "gets" you, even if you know that they don't personally agree with what you have to say?

When you are validated by another person, you know that they really appreciate who you are and what you are trying to achieve. If you are trying to negotiate an outcome or just talk through a difficult situation, validation is a great starting point. It builds rapport and respect.

At this point, I want to draw a clear distinction between empathy and validation. If you have read my other books, you'll know how to use empathy in your relationships. To briefly recap, empathy is the ability to put yourself in the position of someone else in order to understand their perspective.

It's an essential ingredient for a good relationship, because it enables you to work through differences and appreciate your partner as a human being.

Validation takes this one step further.[61] To validate someone is to signal that you not only understand another person's perspective, but that you are happy to accept them exactly as they are.

Rather than summarizing and reflecting their feelings, you provide the individual with concrete reasons why you understand their position.

You not only state that you "hear" or "feel" them, but that you acknowledge their position as valid. Ideally, you will also throw in a couple of reasons why they might feel that way.[62] The most powerful combination of all is empathy combined with a large helping of validation.

Still confused? Let's look at an example of empathy versus empathy plus validation.

Empathy in action

PARTNER: You didn't call me when you said you would. Do you not care about my feelings? I'm feeling hurt right now.

YOU: I hear you. I know that my behavior has really upset you. I'm sorry.

Empathy plus validation in action

PARTNER: You didn't call me when you said you would. Do you not care about my feelings?

YOU: I hear you, and I know that I've upset you. I'm sorry. I know that last month you told me about how bad you felt in your last relationship when your ex took too long to call you back, and I know that I messed up last week too when I got home much later than expected. I can see why it looks like I don't care, and I get why you feel that way. I certainly do care about your feelings, and I'd like to make it up to you.

---

[61] Rodman, S. (2015). *Validation: Beyond Empathy*. huffingtonpost.com
[62] Ibid.

The second response appears much more thoughtful. It isn't defensive, and it's phrased in such a way that the other person feels as though they matter.

Proof that validation really does make a difference

Not convinced? Research attests to the sheer power of validation. For example, in a study run by two Korean psychologists, validation trumped empathic responses when it came to boosting participants' self-esteem and lowering their levels of aggression.[63]

The researchers recruited 80 participants, who were invited to take part in a computer game. Using sneaky computer programming tactics, some participants were made to believe that the other players were excluding them from the game.

The participants were then split into three groups. One group listened to a recording that featured neutral facts about the game.

The second group heard a set of empathic statements that described the feelings they might have experienced when the other players "excluded" them.

Finally, the third group listened to a recording that not only described the feelings they might have experienced, but validated them. For example, the final group heard this statement:

"Seeing that you felt bad in this situation, you probably wish to get along with people and consider a sense of belonging and closeness with others important."

Although both the empathic and validation conditions made the participants feel better about being excluded, the validation condition was more effective.

---

[63] Kim, E., & Kim, C. (2013). Comparative Effects of Empathic Verbal Responses: Reflection Versus Validation. *Journal of Counseling Psychology, 60, 3,* 439-444.

Validation tips

Use guesses if it's not clear what they are feeling: Someone who is experiencing conflicting emotions might not be able to articulate them. Until you both know what's going on, you can't fully validate another person.

Evaluate their words and body language, then use the following phrases to make sensitive, diplomatic guesses:

"It sounds to me as though you feel..."

"From my position, it sounds like your primary emotion right now is..."

"Would you say that you are feeling...?"

It doesn't matter if you are wrong, because the other person can correct you. In fact, it can be helpful for your partner to discover what they are *not* feeling, because it narrows down their possible answers!

As long as you remain patient and validate whatever emotions come up for them, this tactic will work in bringing about a shared understanding.

Ask clarifying questions: If you merely parrot someone's words back to them, along with a couple of generic validating phrases, they will suspect that you didn't really listen to them in the first place.

The solution is to ask one or two questions and listen attentively – even if you already know the answers! – because doing so will make your validating statements appear sincerer.

Let's say that your partner has been involved in several different projects at work. Recently, they have also been making occasional remarks about their manager's incompetence.

PARTNER: Oh my God, I had a terrible day at work! Our team leader won't listen to any of the suggestions we make, even though the project is really starting to come off the rails.

YOU: You sound frustrated. Which project are you referring to?

PARTNER: The upcoming marketing campaign. It's so stressful. There's so much work to be done.

YOU: I can see that this is causing you a whole heap of trouble. Obviously, you feel overwhelmed. That makes total sense, given that you've had to deal with a lot of problems at work recently.

In this kind of conversation, it is important to hone in on precisely what is bothering your partner. If you aren't entirely certain what is causing them so much distress, your attempts at validation and empathy might appear patronizing or impersonal.

Refer back to past events if appropriate. Nothing happens in a vacuum,[64] so if you are puzzled by the strength of your partner's reaction, consider what has happened in the past that may have influenced their view in the present.

Normalize – sometimes: It can be reassuring to know that you aren't the only person in the world to react in a particular way to a situation, and most people appreciate some validating words that let them know that their reaction is normal.

For example, if your friend tells you that they are looking forward to starting a family but feel daunted by the prospect of becoming a parent, you could validate them like this - "That's understandable. Becoming a parent is a big responsibility. I think a lot of people feel as you do." In other words, you are "normalizing" their feelings.

However, there are a couple of circumstances in which it is not appropriate to normalize someone else's emotions. The first circumstance concerns especially

---

[64] Hall, K. (2012). *Understanding Validation: A Way to Communicate Acceptance.* psychologytoday.com

sensitive or traumatic situations. Be very careful in reassuring someone that their feelings are normal, because they may feel as though you are patronizing them. Avoid phrases like "Everyone would feel as you do," or "It's normal to feel like that."

Normalizing isn't a good idea when the other person has behaved in a manner most people would find bizarre or unacceptable.[65]

For instance, if your partner had been written up at work for shouting and swearing at a customer, it wouldn't be appropriate to tell them that anyone would have done the same!

For a start, this simply isn't true. Second, you do not want to risk encouraging or condoning immoral behavior.

Finally, your insincerity may show in your tone of voice or body language. Once someone has realized that you are willing to lie in this kind of conversation, they will be reluctant to trust you in the future.

Match your body language to your words: Even if you pride yourself on your ability to multitask, it's never acceptable to split your attention between your partner and something else whilst offering validation. They will assume that although you are saying all the "right things," you are not really taking the situation seriously.

Refrain from commenting on their choices: Note that validation does not equal agreement. You can hold a totally different view, but still fulfil your partner's need for validation.[66]

However, if you are making judgments about someone else's choices, you are not validating them. In fact, you are doing the complete opposite. I know that keeping a clear head can be hard, but validation and judgment can't go together.

---

[65] Ibid.
[66] Futures Palm Beach. (2017). *DBT Decoded: Validation.* futuresofpalmbeach.com

Take ten minutes alone if you need some time to switch from a judgmental to validating state. If you feel compelled to offer advice, wait until they have finished giving you their account of the situation.

Tell them that as you listened to them speak, you formed an opinion of your own. Ask them whether they would like to hear your suggestions. Never impose your view on anyone.

Think before saying "Me too!:" It can be reassuring and validating to know that someone else has handled a problem you are facing in a similar way. "I would have done the same," or "I did exactly the same thing when that happened to me" can validate someone's choice.

However, you should make sure that your experience really is similar to their own. Otherwise, you could appear insensitive or ignorant.

Don't propose a quick fix: When you care about someone, it's normal to come up with ways to "solve" the problem. However, if you leap in with a solution that you think should make them feel better, the other person might feel invalidated.

Instead of immediately offering to solve the problem, let them work through their feelings first. Most people can figure out for themselves what they need to do.

The purpose of validation is not to act as a superhero, but to adopt the positon of a fellow human being who appreciates their situation.

Watch out for "validation fishing:" We all want validation, but some of us are subtler than others when it comes to asking for it. If your partner is the sort of person who will ask you directly for time and attention, that's great – but not everyone is comfortable voicing their needs.

This means that you'll have to become used to spotting the signs that they are "fishing" for your validation. They will be individual to your partner, but signs that they want your attention and validation include:

1. *Sighing and tutting when they aren't in your line of vision* – they probably want you to turn around and ask them what's wrong.

2. *Glances and looks that aren't accompanied by words.* They might just be checking you out or gazing at you in adoration, but it's probably a sign that they want to talk about an important issue and get some feedback.

3. *They come and sit or stand beside you – but don't actually do anything.* They might simply be enjoying a moment of peace or relaxation, but it's likely that they want to have a conversation and air their feelings.

How to ask someone else for validation

What should you do when you need some validation from your partner? Easy – you ask. OK, it might not be that straightforward.

Lots of us have been raised to believe that making a direct request for validation is wrong and self-centered. I'm here to tell you that it isn't, unless of course you ask your partner for reassurance all the time. Occasionally asking them to validate your feelings and thoughts is healthy and normal.

If this is an alien concept to you, don't worry. Here are a few phrases you can borrow:

"I feel X about Y. Do you think I'm being unreasonable?"

"When X said Y to me, I was very hurt. Would you have felt the same way?"

"I can't believe that X did Y! It's shocking. I don't want to see X again. It's normal to feel upset in this kind of situation, right?"

"I feel really positive that I managed to do X. I didn't think it would be possible. Are you proud of me?"

Remember that asking a question when you don't want to hear the answer is destructive. Only ask if there is a reasonable chance that your partner will be able to offer you the validation you need. If not, talk to someone else.

Self-validation

Just in case you needed another reason to practice validation, think about this – what if you were able to validate yourself whenever you needed some encouragement?

Over the years, I've come to appreciate the importance of positive inner dialogue. You know that inner voice that comments on your actions and feelings all day?

I'm not exaggerating when I say that it can make all the difference when it comes to your success at work, in relationships, and life in general.

If you can't validate your own feelings, you leave yourself vulnerable to depression. In the short term, denying your feelings can help you cope with emotionally draining situations. However, if you leave feelings unprocessed, they can come back to bite you later.

For example, let's say that you ask someone out on a date, and they say "No." You really like this person, so their answer stings. You tell yourself that it didn't really matter, shrug it off, and start joining online dating sites in a bid to distract yourself. The problem? Deep down, their rejection has hurt you. Badly.

In this kind of situation, the healthiest response is to take some time for yourself and acknowledge how you feel. Internal dialogue and self-validation are powerful tools in working through your emotions and moving past painful events.

On the other hand, when you invalidate yourself, you are setting yourself up for long-lasting unhappiness.

Let me show you what self-validation versus self-invalidation look like.[67] Here's some validating internal dialogue:

"This feels awful. Rejection sucks. It's not surprising that I feel this way – I really liked them. At least I know that I'm capable of asking someone out. That took courage. And it's good to know that there are people out there that I really want to be with."

"God, I feel like crying right now. I'm starting to feel as though I'll never find a partner. Given that I had two important relationships end in my twenties, I think this is a reasonable way to feel. Fortunately, I can be happy whilst single. I just need a bit of time."

On the other hand, here's some self-invalidating dialogue:

"Stop moaning. Some people have far worse problems."

"You're a grown man/woman, stop being pathetic."

"Did you really think you stood a chance with them anyway? Get real!"

"I don't know why I'm so upset. There are lots of fish in the sea!"

I think it's obvious that the self-validating dialogue is much more helpful! It sets the stage for positive future action, and it encourages an optimistic outlook.

If you don't believe me, just try it for a few days. Heck, just try monitoring your inner dialogue for 24 hours! I can guarantee you'll feel better about yourself and life in general when you master the art of self-validation.

---

[67] Birch, A. (2016). *Others Have It Worse Than Me: Self-Invalidation.* psychopathsandlove.com

Chapter 12: How to Say "No" To Anyone

In a healthy relationship, both partners will want to please one another. (If you aren't interested in making your partner happy, it's time to rethink your decision to be with them!) Unfortunately, it's possible to take this natural desire too far.

If you don't know when to say "No," you will end up going along with whatever your partner wants, but feeling resentful.

In the long run, if you don't feel as though you can discuss how their requests make you feel, you will resort to passive-aggressive communication in a bid to let them know that you are hurt.

At the start of a relationship, nothing feels too much trouble when it comes to your new partner. When I met my last girlfriend, I offered to come over every morning during a cold spell and shovel snow from her drive!

She thought I was crazy and, in a sense, I was. My brain was completely in thrall to the hormones that were flooding my body.

By the time our second anniversary had rolled around, I probably would have said "No thanks!" if she'd asked me to get up at 6am and clear the driveway. It's not that I'd become a jerk in the meantime, just that our relationship had matured.

As we get to know our partners and become more comfortable, we come back down to earth and take a more realistic view of the relationship. We start weighing up each side of the equation, and take stock of whether the relationship is balanced. We ask ourselves:

1. Do I feel as though my partner does as much for me as I do for them?

2. Is there a "giver" and a "taker" in this relationship?

3. Am I happy with the way things are?

4. If I'm not, is there any way I can change them?

5. Do I feel as though I have a choice regarding what happens in our relationship?

These aren't questions to be taken lightly.

Think of it like this. If you can't say "No," you can never give a meaningful "Yes" either. A relationship in which you cannot make your true wants known is a relationship based on inauthentic communication.

Therefore, you need to understand how to turn down a request. This skill is also invaluable in friendships and business.[68]

I recommend tailoring your strategy to suit the other person's request. To keep it simple, I like to sort requests into "reasonable" and "unreasonable."

Dealing with reasonable requests

Reasonable requests are those that most people would deem normal and appropriate. For example, if your partner asks you to pick them up from the airport at 5pm next Friday and you have flexible working hours, this isn't an outlandish request.

You might still have to say no, but no one would blame them for asking. Most of us are happy to consider reasonable requests from those we love, because they would probably help us out in return.

Let's say that, in this case, you would normally be happy to rearrange your Friday schedule, but it just so happens that you have an unusually busy week. On top of that, one of your most important clients wants to meet with you at 4.30pm Friday

---

[68] Duccio. (2017). *Learning to say No sometimes can be very beneficial.* howtobehappyguru.com

afternoon. In short, you need to turn down your partner's request to collect them from the airport. How might you handle the situation so that both of you go away from the conversation feeling respected?

Open with a positive: If you make the other person feel bad for asking you to help, they will go on the defensive. They might also think twice before asking you for help in the future, which isn't good news for your relationship.

Therefore, it's best to start with a response that will build trust and confidence between you. "I'd really like to, and it always makes me happy to help you out…" would be a strong opener in the above case.

Briefly outline a reason behind the "No" if you can: As the saying goes, "No" is a complete sentence in its own right. However, if the request is reasonable and in good faith, giving a reason is a nice gesture.[69] The best reasons are nonnegotiable.

For example, "I have a meeting which cannot be rescheduled" is a sound reason and a suitably brief explanation.

Offer a link or piece of advice that will help them out or make them feel good: Your partner might not be happy that you can't help them, but an alternative form of support or a kind gesture will help soften the blow.

This tactic will let them feel as though you care (and you do care, right?), even though you can't give them what they originally wanted from you. To continue with the same example, you could offer to order them a taxi, or have their favorite meal waiting for them in the fridge.

Let's look at another example, this time in the context of a friendship. Suppose that your best friend wants you to help her make invitations for her upcoming wedding at the weekend.

---

[69] Levine, I.S. (2011). *7 Tips for saying NO to a friend.* huffingtonpost.com

She isn't sure how to put a handmade invite together, and wants your opinion on color schemes. Unfortunately, you have already promised to visit your parents.

You could give a response along the following lines:

"I'd love to help, but I promised to visit my family weeks ago. I know that Shelly [a mutual friend] loves crafting and I think she's free this weekend – perhaps you could ask her?"

"I'd love to help, but I promised to visit my family weeks ago. I know I can't be there in person to help you out, but I'd be happy to look over a few photos if you want to send them to me."

Both of these approaches allow you to get your own needs met, whilst still helping your friend. Note that this is a "soft no" tactic. It works great if you truly like the other person and want to help them.

However, if you would rather give a straight "No," meeting someone in the middle will leave you feeling resentful. Use the techniques in the next section instead.

End with a note of encouragement: End the conversation or a note with a few warm words that show how much you care.[70]

For example, if your partner has asked you to pick up their son's medicine from the drugstore on your way home from work, but you won't have time, you could tell them that you really hope their son feels better soon and that you are looking forward to seeing them at the weekend.

Don't take responsibility for someone else's reaction: Sometimes, you might experience a little (or a lot) of negative pushback when you tell someone that you can't or won't help them.

---

[70] Franzen, A. (2017). *How to Say No to Anyone (Even a Good Friend).* themuse.com

If you are usually a passive person with a reputation as a people pleaser, others might be surprised. Here's the most important thing to remember – as long as you've been reasonable in your approach, their response really isn't a reflection on you.

Period.

Defend your boundaries and stand up for your right to be seen as more than a servant!

Saying "No" to unreasonable people and requests

The above tips work well when you have a good relationship with the other person, and the request under discussion is reasonable.

Unfortunately, as you know, there are plenty of people in this world who are happy to try their luck and trample over your needs in a bid to make their own lives easier.

For example, let's say that you have taken a week's vacation from work. It's Tuesday, and you aren't due to return until Thursday, but your phone rings – it's your boss!

They acknowledge that you are on vacation, but ask whether you'd be willing to come in the next morning anyway because they are "short on staff." You are hoping for a promotion at work, so you don't want to get on your boss's bad side.

At the same time, you have scheduled a lot of fun activities for the final day of your vacation, and you don't want to get a reputation as a pushover.

What should you do in this kind of position? Here are a few guidelines:

Assert your boundaries by stating "personal rules:" If you are asked to do something that makes you feel uncomfortable or goes against your beliefs, say that your personal code of conduct or behavior means that you cannot help them.

"I have a rule that I don't do X," or "I never do Y" is a firm way of drawing a clear line. If they probe for more information or criticize you for sticking to your standards, say

"These are my personal rules, and I don't make exceptions." You can then say, "I'm glad I can trust you to respect my wishes." This puts subtle pressure on them to behave in a respectful manner. Not many people like to think that they are the sort of person to trample on someone else's boundaries.

Use the broken record technique: This one is a classic for a reason. Repeat the same answer, in the exact same tone of voice, until the other person gets the message.

If you are in a situation that allows for some humor, tell them that you said "no" the first time around, and perhaps they need to get their hearing checked.

Don't fear the silence: When someone calls on you for a favor, it's not your responsibility to take control of the conversation. Once you have provided them with a response, it's their turn to react.

A few moments of silence won't kill you, and there's no need to jump in with unnecessary explanations or apologies to fill it up.

Don't fall into the trap of accepting "gifts:" Some people try to "convince" others to grant them favors by giving or offering an unwanted gift.

I'm not a cynical person by nature, but if someone who doesn't seem to care about you suddenly goes out of their way to offer help or give you a gift, I'd advise you to be on your guard. In all likelihood, they probably want something in return.

The sneakiest people are those who give a gift, wait a week or two, and then pull out their request! Do not take them up on any offers of help, and decline material gifts if possible. On the plus side, you will at least have advance warning of their actions. This gives you a chance to rehearse how you will say "No" to their demands.

Use a noncommittal phrase: This tactic works on people who don't come out and ask for your help directly, but complain about their situation in such a way that it's obvious they expect you to help.

"Oh dear," "What a shame," or "That's a pity" allows you to sympathize without committing yourself to actually helping another person. If they are in desperate need of help, this strategy forces them to spell out what they really want and need.

Give them some praise in advance: End the conversation or message with a short, uplifting note, reassuring them that you are confident in their ability to sort their own problem. This draws a line under the topic, and makes you appear polite and supportive.

How to reject a date

No matter how great your communication skills, and how much relationship experience you have, dating often gets awkward. One of the trickiest situations comes when you have to issue a rejection. It's a special kind of "No," because it feels so personal.

Being on the receiving end of a "No" hurts, but turning someone down isn't much fun either. So, what should you say when someone asks you out, but you just aren't interested?

Express your thanks: It's not easy to ask someone out on a date! In all likelihood, they were nervous about asking you, so bear this in mind when turning them down. There is no excuse for mocking someone. Ever.

Respect their dignity, and thank them for the invitation. Think of your reputation. You don't want to be known as a mean jerk who mocks anyone who dares ask you on a date.

"No, but thank you" is a complete answer: You don't owe anyone a fuller explanation. Don't feel obliged to give them a rundown of why the two of you wouldn't be compatible, why your circumstances aren't ideal, and so on. A straightforward "No" is best in most situations.[71]

---

[71] Allan, P. (2015). *How to Turn Down a Date Gracefully.* lifehacker.com

If you truly like them as a person, you can use a gentler approach: If you are asked out by a friend or colleague you genuinely like – but only as a friend – it's fine to tell them the truth.

"You are a fantastic friend/girl/guy, but I just don't have romantic feelings towards you" will get the point across whilst still affirming your respect for them.[72]

Don't say that you aren't looking for a relationship (unless it's true): Reject that specific date/relationship, not relationships in general.

Otherwise, the person you have rejected might choose to wait and see whether you change your mind rather than move on. They will also become upset if and when you start dating someone else soon after.

Never suggest you may change your mind: How many times have you heard people in movies, TV shows, and even real life tell someone that they'll "think about it"?

I understand why people do this – they don't want to reject someone to their face, or they want to buy themselves a bit of time before delivering the killer blow.[73]

Don't do it. It leaves them hanging on, hoping that you will someone change your mind. Believe me, it's kinder to give a straight "No," then give them the time and space in which to process their disappointment.

The "I'll think about it" strategy doesn't work in your favor, either. When you leave the conversation, you'll start worrying how long you can expect them to wait before accepting that you really aren't interested.

If you have to work or socialize with the other person, things get very awkward very quickly.

---

[72] Kaufman, G. (2013). *3 Guy-Approved Ways to Turn Down a Date Without Hurting His Feelings.* glamour.com
[73] Ibid.

"No" is one of the most important words in the English language, and learning how to use it is the first step in the process to getting what you really want.

"No" isn't selfish. It's an essential tool for anyone who wants to be more honest with themselves and others.

Chapter 13: How to Stop Having the Same Old Arguments

Earlier in the book, I explained that as a relationship matures, it's normal to feel more comfortable with your partner.

This comes with its advantages – you start feeling more secure, and you develop meaningful intimacy – but at this stage, you might start noticing that you fight about the same things over and over again.

This happens to almost every couple. It's not a sign that your relationship is doomed, or that you are incompatible.

It's your job to learn how these dynamics develop, why the same topics come up on a frequent basis, and to develop an arsenal of communication strategies that will help your relationship run more smoothly.

Why do you need to learn how to handle repetitive fights?

When you have the same fights all the time, the joy and trust is slowly sucked from your relationship.

You start to have second thoughts about the relationship, and find yourself thinking things like "We always fight, and it's exhausting," and "Surely it shouldn't be this hard?"

Here's a depressing statistic – 69% of issues that arise in long-term relationships never get resolved![74]

Don't despair – there's some good news! If your personal fighting pattern is predictable, you can learn how to spot the signs and sort out your differences once and for all.

---

[74] Godson, S. (2014). *Perpetual Issues: 69% of disagreements will never be fully resolved so couples need to argue in more effective ways.* suzigodson.com

The secret is to hone your communication skills, and focus on your partner's needs as much as your own.

Before we dive into the strategies that will improve your relationship, here's another statistic that shows precisely why it's so important to improve your fighting style. It'll come as no surprise that the happiest couples have the most positive feelings about their relationships. Obvious, right?

What you might not know is that there is a specific ratio that governs relationship happiness. As a rule of thumb, when a couple experiences five positive conversations or interactions for every negative interaction, they are likely to stay together and enjoy a mutually fulfilling relationship.[75]

Think about that for a moment – you need a whole lot of positive feelings to cancel out just one unhealthy argument. It's in your best interests to sharpen your conflict management skills!

Strategies that prevent and shut down repetitive arguments

Stop resisting: In the introduction, I talked about the unhealthy expectations we have for our relationships. One of these unspoken "rules" is that "Fighting is bad." This isn't true. Fighting is fine. It's fighting dirty that's the problem.

Don't try to solve your problems by pretending that they don't exist, or by making an "anti-fighting pact." It won't work – the problems will still be there, bubbling away under the surface.

Before long, the two of you will start to show your unhappiness through passive-aggressive behavior. Worse, you'll start to feel as though you can't speak up in your own relationship. This will drive you apart.

---

[75] Ibid.

Identify your top three issues: Do this exercise alone and together. Give yourself a few minutes to sit down and think about the issues that cause you the most problems as a couple.

The overlap between your lists will give you an insight into the issues that trip you up. Note that this exercise is NOT intended to give you an arena in which to fight.

You are not aiming to resolve any of the issues right now, just to discover the root cause of your problems. Awareness is the first step to solving the problem.

Identify the underlying feelings behind an argument: Ask yourself, "What's really going on here?" For example, let's suppose you and your partner are fighting about one another's spending habits.

You like to save money and lead a simple life, whereas your partner would prefer to go out for a fancy dinner every week and splash out on expensive vacations.

On one level, this disagreement is about money. However, on another level, something else might be going on.

Your need to save money might be tied to a desire for security, whereas your partner might feel as though buying themselves nice experiences and possessions is the best way of helping themselves relax after yet another week of work.

They might feel that when you ask them to save money, you are treating them like a child. So, the ultimate issues here are security, plus feeling respected as an adult.

How do you tap into the underlying issues? Use "Why" and "How" questions until you drill down to the base of the problem. For example:

PARTNER 1: I feel patronized right now.

PARTNER 2: Why?
PARTNER 1: I don't like the way you tell me to budget more and spend less.

PARTNER 2: *Why?*

PARTNER 1: *Because it makes me feel like a child or an idiot. It makes me feel as though you don't respect me.*

The last line says it all. Although the couple need to reach a compromise on practical financial matters, they also need to address the fact that Partner 1 feels as though there is an underlying power imbalance in the relationship. This kind of conversation paves the way for a discussion about each person's need to feel respected.

Spot the triggers: Every couple has a slightly different fighting style, but there are certain phrases that act as a trigger to large, destructive arguments:

"You always…"

"You never…"

"Why am I always the one to…?"

"I'm just sick of this whole thing, I don't care anymore…"

"We'll never work this problem out…"

What do all these have in common? They are either broad generalizations, which help no one and take your focus away from the problem that is actually under discussion, or they hint at some vague, ominous threat that will put the other party on the defensive.

Never use these phrases. Remember that even if someone uses them against you, you do not have to respond in kind. The best approach is to return to the problem at hand.

I know it takes a lot of willpower to avoid getting dragged into the "You always/No I don't/Yes you do" game, but avoiding it will save you so much trouble in the long run.

Make a physical change: Do you end up using the same words in your arguments, and adopting the same posture? The next time you are having a fight, make a conscious decision to move your body so that you are positioned in a different way.

There is a strong link between our minds and bodies, and physical habits are closely tied in with our thought patterns.[76]

For example, if you tend to sit on the same chair next to the sofa when you have an argument with your partner, shift to the other side of the room and take a new seat instead.

This breaks the chain of associations between how you are feeling, the type of words you are using, and the way you are holding yourself. When you change one of these factors, it becomes easier to change another.

Hone in on specific issues: Have you ever had an argument that was prompted by a minor issue, but then spiraled out of control? Here's an example I remember from my college dating days:

ME: You said you were free on Friday, but now you have to go to your best friend's party?

GIRLFRIEND: Yeah, that's right.

ME: Didn't you know about this in advance? I mean, it's Wednesday now! Surely she asked you ages ago? I've made dinner reservations.

GIRLFRIEND: You're always so fussy. Why can't we go out on Saturday instead?
ME: That's not the point. It's not about the day. It's about the fact you always flake on me.

---

[76] Giang, V. (2015). *The Surprising & Powerful Links Between Posture & Mood.* fastcompany.com

GIRLFRIEND: *Well guess what? You're always annoying me with your stupid schedules.*

This argument started because we were trying to plan our next date, but it soon descended into a fight about what she and I were "always" doing.

As you might have guessed, we ended up shouting at one another about these broader issues rather than actually resolving the problem at hand.

If I'd kept the conversation on track by focusing on the date itself, the fight could have been avoided altogether.

Now, I did have an issue with my girlfriend flaking on me – this wasn't the first time something like this had happened. However, it wasn't the time or place to raise the issue.

Follow this basic rule to stop fights spiraling out of control:

-If you are fighting about something specific, sort out that issue.

-If you feel as though there's a larger underlying problem that needs to be resolved, agree to talk about it another time.

Don't bring up the past: Don't stockpile past arguments and resentments to fling in your partner's face during a fight. It achieves precisely nothing. You'll both feel even angrier and more upset, and your partner will feel insulted that you resorted to such a low tactic.

Agree to disagree: If you want your partner to agree with you on every little thing, you are going to be disappointed. It's a fact of life that those closest to us aren't going to share our frame of reference.

Guess what? Part of being an emotionally mature adult is making allowances for difference. It's healthier to work with how things actually are, rather than wishing they were different and resenting your partner for just being themselves.

Once you've had the same old argument several times over, it's time to reach an agreement for the sake of your relationship. You don't have to "win" every fight. Think about your relationship rather than your ego.

Stop thinking of ways to change your partner's mind. You can't magically change their opinions, but you have a choice when it comes to tolerating their behavior and beliefs.

Painful as it may be, you might come to the conclusion that the two of you are simply incompatible. You will be left with the task of deciding whether to leave the relationship, but at least you will be making decisions based in reality.

Boost the positive: Remember the 5:1 ratio? Tackle your relationship problems from two angles. Take proactive measures to resolve conflict, but don't forget to take preventative measures to stop issues arising in the first place.

Be sure to spend enough time together. Scheduled dates and conversations might not sound romantic, but it's a tried and tested way of making sure that you store up some positivity in your relationship memory bank.

Verbal repair

Here's a simple strategy that can go a long way in soothing your partner's feelings. We don't always fight fair, even when we are trying our best to have a constructive discussion with a loved one.

However, you can make the smart choice and do a little "verbal repair." This will be challenging if you have an ego – and who doesn't? – but just a few words during a heated exchange can prevent long term resentment from building up. These short phrases work as verbal repair. Try these:

"Sorry, let me try a new approach."

"Sorry, I'll rephrase that."

"I know I overreacted. Please let me try again."

"I know I've hurt your feelings. Can I try again?"

"I think I know where I went wrong. Can I explain it in a different way?"

Remember that your tone counts just as much – if not more – than your words.[77] Never use a sarcasm or patronizing tone of voice with your partner. It's better to take a break from the situation if you cannot trust yourself to speak with respect.

What if these strategies don't work?

The advice in this chapter is backed up by solid psychological research, but I appreciate that you might not be able to solve the problem by yourself.
You need to think about getting some professional help if:

1. Your partner doesn't want to work with you to sort out your problems.
2. Your fights turn violent or abusive.
3. Your everyday communication has suffered, i.e. you can't seem to talk about anything anymore.

When a relationship has started to disintegrate, you need to act quickly before its foundations are permanently damaged.

When you repeat the same arguments and neither of you feel heard by the other, one or both partners can slide into apathy. One person can try to carry a relationship for a while, but if one partner has quietly given up, there is little point in carrying on.

The moment you suspect counseling is necessary, book a session with a therapist. Tell your partner why you think the two of you should get help to work on your relationship, and ask them if they would mind coming with you.

---

[77] Harrow, S. (2010). *Stop Fighting! Relationship Repair Without Speaking.* psychologytoday.com

Unfortunately, they might tell you that they don't want to get therapy, or even deny that there is anything wrong. This in itself is a problem – but go to the session anyway.

Therapists are trained in talking to people who are having problems in their relationship, and they can advise you on how to move forward, whether alone or as part of the relationship.

I believe in trying to save relationships, but it's unrealistic to expect that every single partnership can work out. There is no shame in leaving a partner who does not meet your needs, who is abusive, or has given up on the relationship.

Your partner should make you happy, not drag you down! At the end of the day, remember that your needs matter.

Respect yourself and don't stay in a relationship that erodes your mental health!

Chapter 14: Topics Couples Fight About Most Often

By this point, you will appreciate how skills such as validation, assertiveness, shutting down repetitive arguments, and appreciating differences in communication styles can help you tackle virtually any relationship problem.

My aim in this chapter is to give you a few practical tips for resolving some of the most common relationship troubles. Yes, you might have to compromise in some instances, but it's still a far better outcome than fighting and resentment!

So what do couples fight about most often?

One of my favorite psychologists is relationship expert John Gottman. Together with his wife Julie, he runs the Gottman Institute in Seattle. The couple have over 40 years' experience in researching romantic relationships, so they know what they're talking about!

According to Gottman, here are the top five issues couples fight about most often:[78]

1. Physical intimacy
2. Extended family
3. Free time
4. Money
5. Housework

When you look at this list, you'll notice two things:

1. It covers virtually all aspects of everyday life. Although "Career" and "Work" aren't on the list, arguments about money and free time indirectly touch on these topics.

---

[78] Science Of People. (2017). *Why Couples Fight: The Top 5 Issues.* scienceofpeople.com

2. Within these categories, there are dozens of potential subtopics that can form the basis for arguments!

Take "Extended Family." Within this category you have potential problems with parents, in-laws, cousins, aunts, uncles, siblings…it's no wonder that people so often have to deal with "family issues."

Physical intimacy

According to popular stereotypes, it's usually men who have higher libidos, but this isn't always the case. Therapists often come across cases in which wives complain that their husbands are no longer interested in them.[79]

In a mismatched relationship, the person with the higher libido starts to worry that their partner doesn't find them attractive, and the person who isn't so interested in sex can start feeling resentful that they are expected to be physically intimate against their will.

So, how can you bridge the gap?

1. *Play the numbers game:* Therapist Seth Meyers recommends that each person in a mismatched couple rank themselves on a scale of 1 to 10, where 1 is "a naturally low libido" and 10 is "a naturally very high libido."

   When both people know their number and that of their partner, they will stop taking differences in libido personally, and can approach the situation from a calmer, more objective angle.[80]

   For example, if you are a 7 and your partner is a 4, it is unreasonable to expect them to initiate intimacy as often as you would like. However, if they are a 4, it means they do have a sex drive, so this could be a starting point for a mutually beneficial compromise.

---

[79] Rodman, S. (2015). *I Am a Wife Who Wants More Sex Than Her Husband.* drpsychmom.com
[80] Meyers, S. (2013). *How Couples Can Cope with Different Libidos, Sexual Desire.* psychologytoday.com

2. *Schedule intimacy:* Sometimes, both partners' libidos drop due to stress, hectic lifestyles, and other outside factors. Scheduling intimacy may sound unromantic, but it can be a good way of making it a priority again.

3. *Learn what your partner really wants and needs:* It's not easy to talk about sexual desires, but it's essential to a healthy long-term sex life.[81] If you can't face having a discussion in person, why not write letters or emails instead?

    When both people feel heard and validated when it comes to sex, they are more likely to physically engage with one another. This kind of discussion can be used to put together a list or "menu" of activities that both parties are happy to do.

Extended family

Jokes about in-laws are often exaggerated, but they contain a grain of truth. If you think about it, given that so many of us have problems with our own families, it's not a surprise that we often find it hard to fit in with someone else's relations!

Here are a few tips to help smooth over familial tensions:

1. *Take a pre-emptive approach:* As you get to know your partner, tell them about any difficult relations you have, and ask them to share their family history with you. As the saying goes, knowledge is power!

2. *Present a united front:* As and when family problems arise, talk the situation through with your partner and agree what the two of you will do in response.

    Consistency will earn you more respect, so never contradict one another in the presence of family members. Do not ask your partner to choose between

---

[81] Orr, G. (2012). *Can a Relationship Cope with a Difference in Libido?* counselling-directory.co.uk

their family and your relationship – there is always a healthier alternative than making ultimatums.[82]

3. *Think about a family in terms of its history:* When you meet someone's relatives, you aren't just meeting a group of people – you are meeting a long history and set of stories.

   If their dynamics seem unusual or toxic for no good reason, assume that something has happened that set the dynamic in motion.

   Don't assume responsibility for your in-laws' problems, and never assume that you will hear every side of a story. When in doubt, stay neutral. Be slow to take sides.

   You should also bear in mind that every family has its own communication style and customs. If you feel offended by their behavior, talk to your partner – difference in background and upbringing may be to blame.

4. *Get to know your partner's relatives before jumping to conclusions:* Sure, you might never get on well with some members of your extended family. But give them a chance before writing them off. Sometimes, our first (or second) impressions are wrong.[83] Avoid relying on what other people tell you, and get to know them as individuals.

5. *If you don't have to maintain a relationship, it's OK to cut contact:* Unless there are solid legal or moral reasons why you need to remain on speaking terms with a relative, it's OK to remove them from your life. Just because someone is your relative doesn't mean that you shouldn't insist on decent treatment. If they can't or won't respect you and your boundaries, it's time to think about walking away.

---

[82] Family Education. (n.d.). *Ten Basic Rules For Dealing With In-Laws*. familyeducation.com
[83] Ibid.

Free time

A lot of couples find it difficult to balance their working lives, childcare, and free time. It's not uncommon for one partner to feel as though they have no time to themselves.

How can you negotiate the amount of free time you spend alone and together during your days off?

1. *Set aside designated "couple time:"* Agree what is reasonable when it comes to shared time, mark it out on the calendar, and stick to it.

   This will give you both something to look forward to, and shut down the "You don't have time for me!" arguments. Joint activities – or at least, some of them - should be fun.[84]

   For example, painting the living room might be a sensible use of your time, but it probably won't build long-lasting intimacy or fond memories.

2. *Don't question your partner if they want some time alone:* We all need some space in which to collect our thoughts and enjoy our hobbies. Do not interrogate your partner about their activities.

3. *Develop – and talk about - your own interests:* It's unhealthy to spend all your free time with your partner, and it gets boring for both of you after a while.

   Develop at least one separate hobby each. This gives you some breathing room from one another, and also gives you something interesting to talk about!

---

[84] Pascale, R., & Primavera, L. (2017). *Time Together and Time Apart.* psychologytoday.com

Money

This is a problematic area for many couples, and with good reason – the way in which you handle your money has a long-term effect on your lifestyle and financial future. The harsh reality is that if you can't talk to your partner about money, you're going to be in for a bad time.

1. *Get transparent from the beginning:* Financial compatibility is vital for a happy long-term future. Never gloss over financial realities.

    Be clear about the kind of lifestyle you lead from the start of your relationship, and never move in together without first laying all your financial cards on the table and agreeing on who will pay for what.[85]

2. *Talk through hypothetical possibilities:* What happens if one of you gets made redundant, or your financial situation changes in some other way? Avoid stress and uncertainty by talking through possibilities in advance.

3. *Make sure you both have a sense of control:* If someone told you how to spend every cent you owned, you'd soon get resentful. Budget and negotiate so that both parties have some money of their own – even if it's a small sum each month – to use however they please, with no justifications required.[86]

Housework

Not many people enjoy housework, and when one person does more than their fair share (or at least, believes they do more than their fair share!), all hell can break loose. Here's how to ensure a fair divide:

---

[85] McGee, S. (2014). *Seven ways to stop arguing with your spouse about money.* theguardian.com
[86] Ibid.

1. *Establish your priorities:*[87] Do you both like a very clean home, or does one of you have much higher standards than the other? Prepare to meet in the middle regarding what is an "acceptable standard."

   For example, you cannot reasonably expect your partner to clean the bathroom every day if they believe that cleaning it twice a week is enough.

2. *Make a list of all the chores that need doing, and make a schedule:* Once you have established what absolutely must be done every day or week, divide up the chores according to ability and preference. Again, both parties might have to compromise here.

3. *Set up an agreed "housework hour:"* If compiling a schedule feels too much like hard work, you can agree to blitz the house together at a specific time every day.

4. *If your partner doesn't cooperate, only raise the issue at the end of the week:* Set up a new schedule every week, and only review it once every seven days. If your partner isn't keeping to their end of the bargain, use your assertive communication skills and boundaries as necessary.

Remember, every single one of these areas can be tackled using your communication skills toolkit. There are a lot of issues to unpick here, so don't try to resolve all of them overnight!

Choose one or two that bother you most, and set yourself the challenge of addressing them constructively with your partner over the coming week.

---

[87] Stritof, S. (2017). *Chores, Chores, Chores.* thespruce.com

Chapter 15: How to Use Communication to Rebuild Trust & Prevent Jealousy

As we all know, people break one another's trust all too often. Cheating and lying are toxic to any partnership, because they erode feelings of security between two people.

To complicate matters further, jealousy creeps into many relationships – and it often gets worse when one partner has been caught betraying the other.

In this chapter, I'm going to teach you communication strategies that will help your relationship survive betrayal and episodes of irrational jealousy.

Rebuilding trust after infidelity

We all know someone who has cheated or been cheated on, but did you know that, according to Statistic Brain, 14% of married women have cheated on their husbands, and 22% of men have cheated on their wives?[88]

On the plus side, this means that the majority of people don't cheat. On the other hand, it's definitely not an unusual problem.

Some people cheat because they have a sense of entitlement and want some "excitement." Think of the person who notices a new attractive colleague at the office, and decides to have an affair on the basis that it will add some spice to their life.

Another example is the man or woman who feels flattered when a younger person shows them some romantic interest, so they get sucked into an inappropriate situation out of excitement and curiosity.

Occasionally, someone might feel that they are falling in love with a third party, but this isn't actually a common factor in an affair. Most of the time, affairs happen

---

[88] Statistic Brain. (2016). *Infidelity Statistics*. statisticbrain.com

because someone doesn't have the motivation or skills to talk about the underlying problems in their relationship.

Specifically, if you feel as though your relationship is lacking either emotionally or sexually, you might feel inclined to go looking elsewhere if you don't have the ability to talk about the real issue with your partner.[89]

On the plus side, excellent communication skills in a relationship will make it less likely that one or both of you will be unfaithful. But what should you do if it's already happened?

Communication strategies that heal relationships

1. *Make conscious agreements:* Most affairs are easy to define – if you are in a monogamous relationship and your partner sleeps with someone else, it's clear that they have violated a boundary.

    However, things can become murkier when it comes to emotional infidelity or inappropriate flirting. For example, one person might think that flirting online with an attractive single acquaintance is harmless, whereas another may see it as a violation of trust.[90]

    If your situation is in the "ambiguous" camp, create "conscious agreements" to rebuild trust and prevent repeat occurrences in the future. Hammer out the details and put them in writing.

    Be completely clear on what is and isn't OK. Conscious agreements bolster trust because they are proof that both people know what will and will not be tolerated.

---

[89] McClintock, E.A. (2016). *The Real Reasons Why People Cheat.* psychologytoday.com
[90] Weiss, R. (2017). *After Cheating: Restoring Relationship Trust.* psychologytoday.com

You should also set up a schedule of regular communication. This encourages openness and transparency, and will help the betrayed partner feel more secure.

Even if everything appears to be going well, setting aside time for a general "catch up" session each week can foster intimacy, connection, and trust.

2. *Emphasize stability and reliability in all your interactions:* Remember, the best relationships are built on a sense of trust and security. If you have betrayed your partner, you should aim to be as calm, dependable, and stable as possible.

    This means exercising patience at all times, staying true to your word – even in relation to trivial matters – and volunteering information about your schedule.

    If you have been betrayed, you can reasonably expect these behaviors from your partner. If they are truly sorry and want to make amends, they will be eager to make you feel more comfortable.[91]

3. *Choose your confidantes wisely:* It can be hard to know what to do after an affair. To make matters worse, talking to outsiders can add to your confusion.

    People often have strong opinions on infidelity, and their opinions can make you question your own judgment. It is best to keep these problems between yourself, your partner, and people you can trust to listen without passing comment on what you should do next.

4. *Avoid drip feeding, and don't tolerate it in someone else:* To drip feed the truth is to release information in small chunks, in the hope that it will make the other person feel "better" or to make a problem seem less serious than it really is.

    Drip feeding is disrespectful, because it causes the betrayed party to feel hurt on multiple occasions as the truth is gradually released.

---

[91] Meyers, S. (2013). *For the Betrayer: 8 Things You Must Know and Do to Rebuild Trust After an Affair.* huffingtonpost.com

Don't do it – have the guts to answer your partner's questions the first time. How can they trust you if you have a history of holding back vital information?[92] If you are the betrayed party, you need to recognize it as a cowardly communication strategy.

5. *Be prepared to rehash the same conversation:* When someone's trust has been shattered, it can take some time for them to fully absorb the reality of the situation.

    A betrayed partner may think of new questions to ask, or want to hear the same explanation again. If you have broken your partner's trust, staying consistent in your explanations will help rebuild it.

    Never tell them that they "should have moved on by now," as this will cause them to retreat from you. If you have been betrayed, please know that it's normal to want to talk about the affair several times over.

6. *Don't justify the unjustifiable:* If you have betrayed your partner, never insult them by trying to justify your actions. There's a fine line between explaining why you acted as you did – which is an important step in telling your partner the truth – and absolving yourself of blame.

    If you have been betrayed, you do not have to listen to justifications – it is your right to shut down the conversation and insist that you have no interest in listening to their "reasons."

7. *Give it time.* Trust cannot be rebuilt overnight, or within a few weeks. It takes commitment and patience on both sides. Whatever side of the equation you are on, stay honest about your feelings.

---

[92] Weiss, S. (2017). *After Cheating: Restoring Relationship Trust.* psychologytoday.com

If you have been betrayed, you do not have to forgive your partner immediately, and claiming that you have "moved on" when you are still hurting will not do your relationship any favors.

If you have hurt your partner, you need to realize that they will need copious reassurance that you are faithful and remorseful for many months to come. A single apology will not be sufficient.[93] If you feel as though this is too big a burden to carry, or too great a task, the best thing to do is end the relationship.

Only 31% of marriages last when one or both parties have been caught cheating,[94] but good communication can act as a bridge back to a functional relationship.

You may need professional therapy to completely move past an affair, but the strategies in this chapter are a good start.

What about irrational jealousy?

Note that I'm talking about irrational jealousy here. If you suspect that your partner is cheating because you have solid evidence, that's not irrational! I'm talking about pointless obsession that has no basis in reality.

So how can you overcome this problem?

1. *Don't overcompensate or over-explain:* If you are faced with a jealous partner, don't fall into the trap of reassuring them multiple times a day that you are faithful, or explaining in exhaustive detail where you have been and what you have been doing.

    This will merely lead you to resent your partner, and it won't satisfy them anyway – someone who is irrationally jealous won't be convinced by logic and reason.

---

[93] Gaspard, T. (2016). *Learning to Love Again After an Affair*. gottman.com
[94] Ibid.

If you are the jealous partner, realize that trust is a choice. You can never prove your partner's fidelity, just as they can't prove yours.

2. *Look for any underlying causes, and discuss them:* Some people find it hard to trust following a bad relationship or an abusive childhood that left them feeling insecure. Talking through these issues can help both parties gain a new understanding of the jealous partner's feelings.

3. *Ask a trusted friend for an outsider's perspective:*[95] If you aren't sure whether your partner is being unreasonable – whether you are the jealous one or not – ask someone you can rely upon to give you their verdict. Sometimes we can get so caught up in this kind of problem that we lose perspective.

4. *Don't allow obsessing to become a hobby:* If you are very jealous, you probably have too much time on your hands. Try good old-fashioned distraction.

If you are the partner of a jealous person, support them in finding new outlets for their mental energy. However, be careful not to patronize them with phrases like "You need to just stop thinking about it." Be diplomatic.

Jealousy can usually be tackled pretty easily if you know how to handle the problem.

However, I'll end this chapter on a cautionary note. If your partner is excessively jealous to the point of causing you significant stress, they may need professional help in order to move past this psychological problem.

Encourage them to seek assistance from a therapist. If they are unwilling to do so, it may be a sign that they place their feelings above yours, which does not bode well for the future of your relationship.

---

[95] Abell, S. (2010). *How can I stop being so jealous?* telegraph.co.uk

Chapter 16: Communication Tools That Will Rekindle the Flame in Romantic Relationships

Love tends to move from passion to a steady bond over time, but that doesn't mean you have to settle for boredom!

In this chapter, I'm going to give you a few quick tips that will fire up the bond between yourself and your partner. **The key takeaway is this – meaningful communication can increase intensity, which can rekindle the "spark."**

Here's how you can breathe life into a relationship that feels somewhat stale:

Give meaningful compliments: When was the last time you told your partner that they looked hot, or that they were doing fantastically well at work? It takes only a couple of seconds to give a compliment, but they can make someone feel appreciated and respected.

Watch out for negative remarks: Along with increasing the number of positive comments you make, check in with yourself and take an inventory of the criticisms and unhelpful remarks you make on a day to day basis.

If you need to raise an issue with your partner, do it in a civil and loving way. Do not make snide remarks or engage in passive-aggressive communication.

Make "love vows:"[96] Relationships need to be balanced. Both parties need to give and take. Restore the balance by making three "love vows" for the next week or month.

Both of you should think of three loving things to do for your partner, and then promise that you'll do them within a specific time frame. For example, you could promise to give them a massage or cook their favorite meal.

---

[96] Barnes, Z. (2016). *Couple's Therapist Explains 11 Ways To Keep The Spark Alive In A Long-Term Relationship.* self.com

Allocate time to talk about boring or mundane issues such as bills and housework: When you settle into everyday life as a couple, you might feel as though your love is crushed under the weight of everyday life.

Set aside an hour or two a week to talk about strictly practical matters. This will free you up to have more fun at other times!

Write a sincere letter that lists what you most admire about them[97]*:* A heartfelt letter is one of the best gifts to give or receive. Such letters encourage mutual intimacy, and make the receiver feel loved and secure in the relationship. I can attest that this works wonders!

In my first serious relationship, I wrote my girlfriend a letter like this four times each year for three years. We are still on positive terms today, and she still thanks me for "being so romantic."

Write gratitude lists and swap them every week: I was once in a relationship with a woman who told me one day that I "didn't appreciate her." I immediately drew up a list of five things she had done for me over the past week – including vacuuming my spare bedroom, and buying me a new phone charger – and presented it to her, along with a sincere declaration of love.

She was shocked, albeit in a good way! She and I got into the habit of writing little "gratitude lists" and swapping them every couple of weeks. I'd recommend this exercise to anyone! Don't forget to include the things we often take for granted.

For example, let your partner know how much you love their hugs, or how much you love the sound of their laugh. In fact, you could make a whole list devoted to the "small stuff" that makes you smile every day.

Communicate across multiple channels: Mix things up! If you usually chat via instant messaging apps, send an email instead. If you don't often use video chat, make

---

[97] WebMD. (2017). *How to Rekindle the Spark in Your Relationship.* webmd.com

a couple of calls next week. Trying new things shows your partner that you are still interested in connecting with them in different ways.

Shut down outside communication for an hour each day: The internet is a wonderful tool, and smartphones are awesome – but obsessive phone use isn't good for your relationship. **To build intimacy and make it easy to really listen to one another, try a phone-free hour at least a couple of evenings each week!**

Make a point of being on your best behavior: You probably made sure that you displayed good manners during the early weeks and months of your relationship, because you wanted to impress your new partner.[98]

Why not relive those early days? They will feel flattered that you are going to such an effort!

We're all guilty of taking people for granted sometimes, but it's pretty easy to make your partner feel good again. If they ask why you are being so nice, tell them the truth!

Apologize for putting in less effort than you did in earlier stages of the relationship, and explain that you want them to feel loved. You don't need an excuse to show your partner how much they mean to you.

---

[98] Wachter, A., & Legallet, S.J. (2015). *5 Ways to Rekindle the Spark in Your Relationship.* huffingtonpost.com

Chapter 17: Effective Communication for Parents & Caregivers

In this chapter, I want to share some extra advice and tips for parents and anyone who works with children and teenagers. I've spent plenty of time minding my two young nephews, and I can tell you that this advice makes childcare a whole lot easier!

How to communicate with any child

We've all been there. You're trying to convince a child to do something – whether it be finishing their dinner, putting their boots on, or going to bed – and they just aren't cooperating. Or maybe you are trying to get through to a teen who doesn't want to talk to you. Whatever their age, communicating with kids can be tough.

Here are some solid principles to follow:

1. *Yelling is pointless:* Yelling may feel good at the time, but it's destructive. It teaches a child that it's OK to shout and act in an aggressive manner when they feel angry, which isn't good!

    Yelling also puts both of you on the defensive, triggering your nervous systems and escalating the situation. This shuts down all lines of communication, which isn't the result you want![99]

    Worse, a child who is yelled at by their caregivers is at greater risk of developing behavioral and social problems.[100]

2. *Give a child some choice:* Children often get frustrated because adults always tell them what to do and how to act. Part of growing up is learning to establish a separate sense of self, and it's hard to do that if you don't have any autonomy.

---

[99] Entin, E. (n.d.) *A Parental Wake-Up Call: Yelling Doesn't Help.* parents.com
[100] Ibid.

Compromise by guiding the child's behavior, but offering them an element of choice at the same time. For example, a child has to get dressed in the morning – but you could offer them the choice of a blue, green, or yellow shirt.

Stay consistent – don't give a child a choice of clothes one morning then not the next, because they will become confused.[101]

3. *Talk during transition times:* Children and teens often feel more relaxed during car trips, when walking to or from a scheduled activity, or when completing mundane chores like helping with the laundry.

   This makes them more likely to open up about issues that are bothering them.[102] Pay extra attention during these moments and be sure to let them speak.

   I was taking my nephew to soccer practice one day, when he casually mentioned that he was upset about his parents' recent separation.

   Until that point, everyone had assumed he was handling it well. I told his mother about our conversation, and my nephew received the counseling he needed.

4. *Let children make their own mistakes:* You might want to pass your hard-earned wisdom onto your children, but it's better to let them find their own way in the world.

   You don't like it when someone tries to interfere in your life, right? Extend the same courtesy to kids, especially teens.

   Obviously, you need to intervene if they are in danger, but most of the time it's best to let them learn from experience. Refrain from giving unsolicited advice.

---

[101] Leyba, E. (2016). *5 Guidelines for Giving Kids Choices.* psychologytoday.com
[102] Taffel, R. (2014). *7 Powerful Tips for Great Parent-Child Communication.*

If your child seems receptive to your opinion, assure them that you recognize the differences between their life and your own.[103]

5. *Show them how to open up about emotions:* Show kids how emotionally balanced people talk about everyday events.[104]

   For instance, if you are feeling annoyed because you had a hard day at work, don't pretend that everything's fine. This will just confuse a child, make them doubt their own judgment, and encourage them to keep their own emotions bottled up.

   Tell the child, in age-appropriate language, why you feel bad. Let them know what happened to you that day, and how you are going to solve the problem.

   This kind of modeling teaches them that it's OK to talk about feelings, and that even the "bad stuff" can be worked out in the end.

6. *Don't patronize a child:* You're the adult, so you know best - right? Not necessarily! Kids can be remarkably perceptive, and they – not you – know how they are thinking and feeling.

   When your child starts talking about their worries or concerns, switch into full listening mode. Do not interrupt and let them explain exactly what is on their mind.[105]

7. *Listen in a nonjudgmental manner:* If you seize every chance to berate your child for their mistakes, they won't feel comfortable opening up to you in the future.

   Impose consequences for bad behavior, spell out rules, and defend your boundaries – but withhold moral judgments where possible.

---

[103] Ibid.
[104] Ibid.
[105] American Psychological Association. (n.d.). *Communication tips for parents.* apa.org

Do you know what teens want most from the adults in their lives? **According to research, they want their parents to be available for important conversations, and to hold back on making quick judgments.**[106]

You won't agree with all your child's views and choices – and that's perfectly OK! Keep your ego in check and be open to the possibility that there is more than one way of looking at a situation.

8. *If you aren't sure what they need from a conversation, just ask:* If a child starts talking to you but the conversation doesn't seem to be going in any particular direction, gently ask whether they want someone to listen, whether they want some advice, or whether they need something else entirely. Just like adults, children and teens vary in their ability to voice their needs.

9. *Open with thoughts rather than questions:* Questions definitely have a place when you're communicating with a child, but too many questions can make them defensive. Sometimes, it's best to open with a thought rather than a query.

For example, if a teen seems particularly distant one Saturday evening but doesn't seem in the mood to talk, you could say "I've been thinking, today has felt a bit slow and dull," and see whether it prompts them to open up.

This approach feels less invasive than questions like "What's the matter?" or "Why won't you talk to me?"

Oh, and it's best to avoid asking questions during dinner too.
If you get into the habit of making every dinnertime into an interview, your children (especially teens) will start dreading it, which will result in a tense atmosphere.

---

[106] Sharma, V. (2000). *Tips for Parent-Child Communication.* mindpub.com

10. *Look beyond irrational statements:* When a child says something like "I hate school!" or "I hate my so-called best friend!" don't respond with a minimizing statement like "Don't be silly," or "I'm sure you don't mean that."

    Instead, validate their feelings and use simple questions to get to the heart of the issue. Asking "Why, exactly?" or "What has happened?" will give you the bigger picture. Their "silly" statements might not be silly after all![107]

11. *Explain the logic behind your decisions:* As a parent or caregiver, you will need to lay down the law from time to time and make decisions.

    However, rather than use phrases like "Because I said so, that's why!," explain the logic behind your decision.

    Even if the child doesn't agree with you, they will at least realize that you have your reasons, and aren't just out to make them unhappy. Show that you have taken time to consider a request, as this will help your child feel respected.[108]

    For example:

    CHILD: Can I go to Stacey's house for a sleepover Friday night?

    PARENT: I'll have to think about that and get back to you in a few minutes, OK?

    [10 minutes later]

    PARENT: I know you love going to Stacey's house and that sleepovers are fun, but we have to visit your aunt on Saturday morning and you'll be tired from the sleepover if you go, so it's a "No" this time.

    CHILD: But I want to go!

---

[107] PBS Parents. (n.d.). *Talking with Kids*. pbs.org
[108] Ibid.

PARENT: I know it's disappointing. But there's a good reason why you can't go, and that's my final answer.

The main rule is to show your child the same respect you would want to receive in return. At the same time, your job is to enforce reasonable boundaries and stick to them.

Contrary to what you might think, children appreciate structure and routine. The best parents are those who use a consistent approach when it comes to discipline, and insist on appropriate standards of behavior. At the same time, they always let their children know that they are there for support and guidance when necessary.

Chapter 18: Communication Strategies for Friendships

Although our romantic relationships tend to be the most intense bonds we make outside our birth families, friendships come a close second.

In fact, some people would argue that losing a long-term friendship can cause more pain than the loss of a long-term romantic relationship. Research has shown that women tend to take "friend breakups" especially hard.[109]

What's the solution? Yep, you've guessed it – communication! Some friendships just aren't destined to last the distance, but knowing how to handle common friendship problems will strengthen your bond and keep you close.

I'm going to talk about three issues that often come up in friendships, and how you can prevent them driving you apart.

Problem 1 – One-Sided Friendships

One-sided relationships are painful. When you feel as though you are putting a lot of effort into a friendship only to receive little in return, you might start to lose your sense of self-worth and confidence.

If you haven't been friends with someone for very long, the best strategy is to cut them loose. But I know this isn't so easy to do if you've been friends for years. I've been in this situation myself. One of my best friends from college, Tom, still hung out with me every couple of weeks for years after we graduated.

The problem was that I always had to initiate contact, which made me feel resentful. He meant a lot to me, so I couldn't bring myself to cut him out of my life – and he was fun to hang out with when we did get together.

So how should you handle this kind of friendship?

---

[109] Leverant, Z. (n.d.). *Does breaking up with a friend hurt as much as ending a romantic relationship?* hopesandfears.com

1. *Tell them how you feel:* You'd think that two friends would notice when their relationship falls out of balance, but some people are just oblivious.[110] What's more, once you get into a routine where someone always arranges everything, the less proactive friend starts to accept that this is "how things are."

   When I worked up the courage to tell Tom how I felt, he was genuinely surprised. He thought that I liked playing the role of organizer! He started to make more of an effort after that conversation, and I began to feel a lot better.

2. *If they have turned distant, get the facts:* If your friend has been unusually distant and out of contact, it's possible that they are facing significant problems in their personal life.

   Be careful. Avoid jumping to conclusions. Don't make them defensive by asking why they haven't been in touch.

   Instead, tell them that you hope they are OK, and that you miss them. Then suggest that the two of you meet. You'll find out pretty quick whether they have been neglecting your friendship through laziness or through circumstance.[111]

3. *Use the power of scheduling:* When hanging out with a friend, ask if you can set up your next hangout before you part ways. Tell them that you've really enjoyed spending time together, and choose a date that works for you both.

   You will no longer have to worry about who will next reach out to make the next "friend date." Just check in the day before and make sure they are still available. Of course, if they keep bailing on you, it's probably time to let the friendship go.

---

[110] Seriously, Sarah? (2015). *How to Deal with One Sided Friendships.* seriouslysarah.net
[111] Goldsztajn, I. (2015). *One-sided Friendships: How to Deal.* hercampus.com

Problem 2 – Jealousy

We'd all like to think that our friends would be happy for us if we got a promotion, bought a new house, got married, or landed our dream job. Unfortunately, jealousy is common among friends. Try these tips:

1. *Tell them the full story:* When someone is jealous of you, they often assume that your life is perfect and that you are totally happy. They get so caught up in what they don't have that their perspective gets warped.

    Make sure they know that you still have your share of problems, and let them know that no situation is truly perfect. For instance, if you are getting married and your friend is jealous, you could casually mention that your in-laws are causing you trouble and that wedding planning is stressful.

    Don't lie or over-emphasize your problems. Just let them know that you have ups and downs, even though your life has changed for the better.

2. *Include them in your joy:* Have you bought a house? Invite your friend over for a special housewarming dinner. Have you just had a baby? Ask your friend to be a godparent. Just got a new job? Ask them to help you pick out a couple of new outfits for your first day.

    Be sure to tell them how much you appreciate their help, and how glad you are that you have friends who can share in your good news.[112] This tactic will help them feel more secure.

3. *Take on the more active role in your friendship for a few weeks:* Jealous people often feel that someone else's good news means that they are suddenly less important. Some extra attention can help reassure an envious friend.

---

[112] Orbuch, T. (2016). *Caught Between a Friend and an S.O.? Here's What to Do.* greatist.com

Make sure that you ask them what's going on in their life, make a special effort to see them regularly, and throw them a few sincere compliments. Don't talk about your good news to the exclusion of everything else, as even the most tolerant of your friends will get sick of it fast.

Suggest a couple of new activities for the two of you to try. See the problem as an opportunity to enliven your friendship.

Problem 3 – Violations of Trust

Most of us have had to deal with a gossiping friend at some point, or someone who has spilled a deeply personal secret. When someone has abused your trust, it's hard to feel close to them again. What should you do when a friend has betrayed you?

1. *Find out why they acted as they did:* Don't try to ignore the problem. You cannot hope to trust someone again unless you know the full story. Sit down with your friend, explain what you know, and ask them for their side of the story.

    Unfortunately, they may deny that anything untoward has happened, which puts you in the position of having to decide whether or not to continue with the friendship.

    On the other hand, you may discover that they didn't realize you wanted a certain piece of information to be kept a secret, or that you have misunderstood the situation.

    Do not rely on third parties to tell you the truth. Go straight to the source. Just as you would with any sensitive conversation, focus on actions and consequences, not personalities.

2. *Brace yourself for defensiveness:* Few people like to think of themselves as backstabbers, so there's a chance that your friend will go on the defensive.

They might even bring up the past and remind you of your own faults in an effort to divert your attention away from the present.

Remain calm, and give them no further ammunition. Focus on the facts. You can work out how you are going to handle the relationship later.[113]

3. *Clean up the damage:* If your so-called friend has been spreading untruths or secrets around, you might need to hold a few conversations with other people.

   For example, if you have reason to believe that your friend has told a third party that you don't like them, you will need to clear the air.

   Ideally, the person who betrayed you will make amends, but it rarely works out that way. Be prepared to take an inventory of the damage and go on a cleanup mission.

   Remember that it takes long-term action to repair a reputation. You may have to model ethical, consistent behavior to regain the trust of others if your reputation has been damaged.[114]

   Draw on a couple of people you can trust at this time, because you'll need moral support.

Should you forgive your friend?

It's up to you whether you want to forgive a friend for their bad behavior. No one is perfect. Try answering these questions to help you decide whether to save the friendship:

1. On the whole, has this friendship influenced your life for the better?

2. Do you have plenty of happy memories with this person?

---

[113] Chua, C. (2017). *Backstabber Guide: 8 Tips to Deal with Backstabbers.* personalexcellence.co
[114] Ibid.

3. Do the two of you support one another on a frequent basis?

4. Would you miss this person a lot if you ended the friendship?

5. Do you feel as though you can talk through your problems with this person?

6. Do you feel as though they are basically a person of good character who has made a mistake?

The more "Yes" answers you can give, the better. On the other hand, there is no law stating that you must stay friends with those who treat you badly.

Only you can weigh up the pros and cons when it comes to cutting ties with people who have hurt you.

Conclusion

You've now learned everything you need to know about finding and keeping a great relationship! I've crammed a lot of tips and tricks into this guide, so don't worry if it feels a little overwhelming right now. You might want to highlight the parts that are most relevant to your relationship, and then read them again at a later date.

Let's recap what you've learned:

1. What a healthy relationship looks like, and how our society sets us up to have unrealistic ideas about love and romance.

2. Why you are bound to fight with your partner from time to time, and how to handle the most common problems people come up against in relationships.

3. How to get into the right mindset for dating, pick the right partner for you, and avoid codependent relationships.

4. How to work out what you do and don't want in a relationship, how to stand up for yourself, and how to say "No" when it matters.

5. How to keep a long-term relationship exciting and fresh.

6. How to communicate effectively with friends, family members, and children.

Impressive, huh?

If you are already in a romantic relationship, you and your partner will start to notice the difference within days if you implement the advice in this book.

If you are single, you can embark on your quest for romance secure in the knowledge that you have at your disposal the ultimate relationship toolkit.

The most important message of all

A relationship takes two people to make it work, and the best relationships are between two individuals with high levels of self-esteem. YOU are a worthwhile person in your own right, and you deserve respect from both yourself and those around you. Live by this rule, and you'll be able to avoid destructive relationships and find real, lasting love.

It's my hope that everyone reading this book will be able to fix their relationship problems using the theories and practical strategies I've offered within these pages.

At the same time, I realize that not all relationship issues can be solved without professional help.

However, even if you do need therapy, this book will still help you strengthen your bond. It will also help prevent problems cropping up again in the future.

I wish you the best of luck – I know you can build the relationship you deserve. May you find your own happy ending!

One last thing before you go. Can I ask you a favor? I need your help! If you enjoyed this book, could you please share your experience on Amazon and write an honest review? It will be just one minute of your time (I will be happy even with one sentence!), but a GREAT help for me.

Since I'm not a well-established author and I don't have powerful people and big publishing companies supporting me, I read every single review and jump around with joy like a little kid every time my readers comment on one of my books and give me their honest feedback!

If I was able to inspire you in any way, please let me know! It will also help me get my books in front of more people looking for new ideas and useful knowledge. If you did not enjoy the book or had a problem with it, please don't hesitate to contact me at contact@mindfulnessforsuccess.com and tell me how I can improve it to provide more value and more knowledge to my readers. I'm constantly working on my books to make them better and more helpful.

Thank you and good luck! I believe in you and I wish you all the best on your new journey!

Your friend,

Ian

My Free Gift to You – <u>Get One of My Audiobooks for Free!</u>

If you've never created an account on Audible (the biggest audiobook store in the world), **you can claim one free** audiobook **of mine**!

It's a simple process:

1. Pick one of my audiobooks on Audible:

http://www.audible.com/search?advsearchKeywords=Ian+Tuhovsky

2. Once you choose a book and open its detail page, click the orange button "Free with 30-Day Trial Membership."

3. Follow the instructions to create your account and download your first free audiobook.

Note that you are NOT obligated to continue after your free trial expires. You can cancel your free trial easily anytime and you won't be charged at all.

Also, if you haven't downloaded your free book already:

Discover How to Get Rid of Stress & Anxiety and Reach Inner Peace in 20 Days or Less!

To help speed up your personal transformation, I have prepared a special gift for you!

Download my full, 120 page e-book "Mindfulness Based Stress and Anxiety Management Tools" for free by clicking here.

Link:

tinyurl.com/mindfulnessgift

Hey there like-minded friends, let's get connected!

Don't hesitate to visit:
-My Blog: www.mindfulnessforsuccess.com
-My Facebook fanpage: https://www.facebook.com/mindfulnessforsuccess
-My Instagram profile: https://instagram.com/mindfulnessforsuccess
-My Amazon profile: amazon.com/author/iantuhovsky

Recommended Reading for You

If you are interested in Self-Development, Psychology, Social Dynamics, PR, Soft Skills, Spirituality and related topics, you might be interested in previewing or downloading my other books:

Communication Skills Training: A Practical Guide to Improving Your Social Intelligence, Presentation, Persuasion and Public Speaking

Do You Know How to Communicate With People Effectively, Avoid Conflicts and Get What You Want From Life?

...It's not only about what you say, but also about WHEN, WHY and HOW you say it.

Do The Things You Usually Say Help You, Or Maybe Hold You Back?

Have you ever considered **how many times you intuitively felt that maybe you lost something important or crucial, simply because you unwittingly said or did something, which put somebody off?** Maybe it was a misfortunate word, bad formulation, inappropriate joke, forgotten name, huge misinterpretation, awkward conversation or a strange tone of your voice?
Maybe you assumed that you knew exactly what a particular concept meant for another person and you stopped asking questions?
Maybe you could not listen carefully or could not stay silent for a moment? **How many times have you wanted to achieve something, negotiate better terms, or ask for a promotion and failed miserably?**

It's time to put that to an end with the help of this book.

Lack of communication skills is exactly what ruins most peoples' lives.
If you don't know how to communicate properly, you are going to have problems both in your intimate and family relationships.

You are going to be ineffective in work and business situations. It's going to be troublesome managing employees or getting what you want from your boss or your clients on a daily basis. Overall, **effective communication is like an engine oil**

which makes your life run smoothly, getting you wherever you want to be. There are very few areas in life in which you can succeed in the long run without this crucial skill.

What Will You Learn With This Book?

-What Are The **Most Common Communication Obstacles** Between People And How To Avoid Them
-How To Express Anger And Avoid Conflicts
-What Are **The Most 8 Important Questions You Should Ask Yourself** If You Want To Be An Effective Communicator?
-**5 Most Basic and Crucial** Conversational Fixes
-How To Deal With Difficult and Toxic People
-Phrases to **Purge from Your Dictionary** (And What to Substitute Them With)
-The Subtle Art of **Giving and Receiving Feedback**
-Rapport, the **Art of Excellent Communication**
-How to Use Metaphors to **Communicate Better** And **Connect With People**
-What Metaprograms and Meta Models Are and How Exactly To Make Use of Them To **Become A Polished Communicator**
-How To Read Faces and **How to Effectively Predict Future Behaviors**
-How to Finally Start **Remembering Names**
-How to Have a Great Public Presentation
-How To Create Your Own **Unique Personality** in Business (and Everyday Life)
-Effective Networking

Direct link to Amazon Kindle Store:

https://tinyurl.com/IanCommSkillsKindle

Paperback version on Createspace:

http://tinyurl.com/iancommunicationpaperback

The Science of Effective Communication: Improve Your Social Skills and Small Talk, Develop Charisma and Learn How to Talk to Anyone

Discover the powerful way to transform your relationships with friends, loved ones, and even co-workers, with proven strategies that you can put

to work immediately on improving the way you communicate with anyone in any environment.

From climbing the career ladder to making new friends, making the most of social situations, and even finding that special someone, communication is the powerful tool at your disposal to help you achieve the success you truly deserve.

In <u>The Science of Effective Communication</u>, you'll learn how to develop and polish that tool so that no matter who you are, where you go, or what you do, you'll make an impact on everyone you meet for all the right reasons.

Discover the Secrets Used By the World's Most Effective Communicators

We all know that one person who positively lights up any room they walk into, who seem to get on with everyone they meet and who lead a blessed life as a result.

Yet here's something you may not know:

Those people aren't blessed with a skill that is off-limits to the rest of us.

You too can learn the very same techniques used by everyone from Tony Robbins to Evan Carmichael to that one guy in your office who everyone loves, and put them to work in getting what you want - without bulldozing over everyone in your path.

Step-by-Step Instructions to Supercharge Your Social Confidence

<u>The Science of Effective Communication</u> is a fascinating, practical guide to making communication your true super power, packed with expert advice and easy-to-follow instructions on how to:

- Retrain your brain to develop powerful listening skills that will help you build better relationships with anyone and gain more value from your conversations.
- Make your voice more attractive to potential romantic partners.
- Mend broken relationships with family members, partners, and even work colleagues.
- Get your views heard by those in authority without being disrespectful.
- Thrive in any job interview and get that dream job.

Your Complete Manual for Building Better Relationships With Everyone You Meet

Bursting with actionable steps you can use IMMEDIATELY to transform the way you communicate, this compelling, highly effective book serves as your comprehensive guide to better communication, revealing exclusive tips to help you:

- Overcome 'Outsider Syndrome,' make friends, and flourish in any social situation
- Keep conversations flowing with anyone
- Make long-distance relationships not only work, but positively prosper

- Reap huge rewards from a digital detox

And much, much more.

Direct Buy Link to Amazon Kindle Store:
http://getbook.at/EffectiveCommunication

Paperback version on Createspace:
http://getbook.at/EffectiveCommPaper

Emotional Intelligence Training: A Practical Guide to Making Friends with Your Emotions and Raising Your EQ

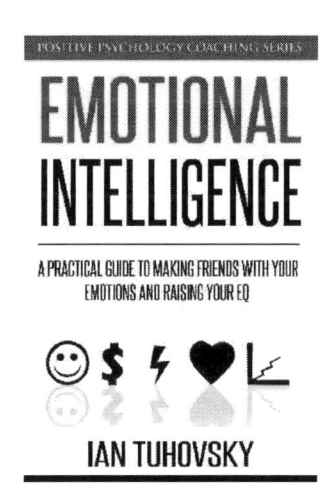

Do you believe your life would be healthier, happier and even better, if you had more practical strategies to regulate your own emotions?
Most people agree with that.
Or, more importantly:
Do you believe you'd be healthier and happier if everyone who you live with had the strategies to regulate their emotions?

...Right?

The truth is not too many people actually realize what EQ is really all about and what causes its popularity to grow constantly.

Scientific research conducted by many American and European universities prove that the **"common" intelligence responses account for less than 20% of our life achievements and successes, while the other over 80% depends on emotional intelligence.** To put it roughly: **either you are emotionally intelligent, or you're doomed to mediocrity, at best.**
As opposed to the popular image, emotionally intelligent people are not the ones who react impulsively and spontaneously, or who act lively and fiery in all types of social environments.
Emotionally intelligent people are open to new experiences, can show feelings adequate to the situation, either good or bad, and find it easy to socialize with other

people and establish new contacts. They handle stress well, say "no" easily, realistically assess the achievements of themselves or others and are not afraid of constructive criticism and taking calculated risks. **They are the people of success.** Unfortunately, this perfect model of an emotionally intelligent person is extremely rare in our modern times.

Sadly, nowadays, **the amount of emotional problems in the world is increasing at an alarming rate.** We are getting richer, but less and less happy. Depression, suicide, relationship breakdowns, loneliness of choice, fear of closeness, addictions—this is clear evidence that we are getting increasingly worse when it comes to dealing with our emotions.
Emotional intelligence is a SKILL, and can be learned through constant practice and training, just like riding a bike or swimming!

This book is stuffed with lots of effective exercises, helpful info and practical ideas.
Every chapter covers different areas of emotional intelligence and shows you, **step by step**, what exactly you can do to **develop your EQ** and become the **better version of yourself**.
I will show you how freeing yourself from the domination of left-sided brain thinking can contribute to your inner transformation—**the emotional revolution that will help you redefine who you are and what you really want from life!**

In This Book I'll Show You:

- What Is Emotional Intelligence and What Does EQ Consist of?
- How to **Observe and Express** Your Emotions
- How to **Release Negative Emotions** and **Empower the Positive Ones**
- How to Deal with Your **Internal Dialogues**
- How to **Deal with the Past**
- **How to Forgive** Yourself and How to Forgive Others
- How to Free Yourself from **Other People's Opinions and Judgments**
- What Are "Submodalities" and How Exactly You Can Use Them to **Empower Yourself** and **Get Rid of Stress**
- The Nine Things You Need to **Stop Doing to Yourself**
- How to Examine Your Thoughts
- **Internal Conflicts** Troubleshooting Technique
- The Lost Art of Asking Yourself the Right Questions and **Discovering Your True Self!**
- How to Create Rich Visualizations
- LOTS of practical exercises from the mighty arsenal of psychology, family therapy, NLP etc.
- **And many, many more!**

Direct Buy Link to Amazon Kindle Store:
https://tinyurl.com/IanEQTrainingKindle
Paperback version on Createspace: https://tinyurl.com/ianEQpaperback

Self-Discipline: Mental Toughness Mindset: Increase Your Grit and Focus to Become a Highly Productive (and Peaceful!) Person

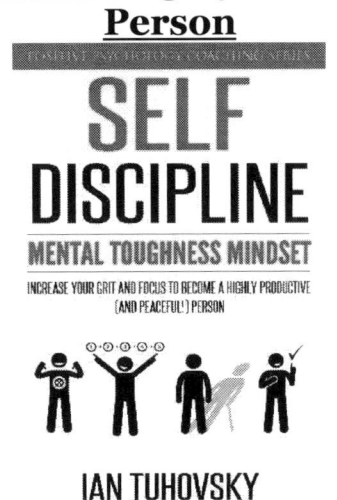

This Mindset and Exercises Will Help You Build Everlasting Self-Discipline and Unbeatable Willpower

Imagine that you have this rare kind of power that enables you to maintain iron resolve, crystal clarity, and everyday focus to gradually realize all of your dreams by consistently ticking one goal after another off your to-do list.

Way too often, people and their minds don't really play in one team.

Wouldn't that be profoundly life-changing to utilize that power to make the best partners with your brain?

This rare kind of power is a mindset. The way you think, the way you perceive and handle both the world around you and your inner reality, will ultimately determine the quality of your life.

A single shift in your perception can trigger meaningful results.

Life can be tough. Whenever we turn, there are obstacles blocking our way. Some are caused by our environment, and some by ourselves. Yet, we all know people who are able to overcome them consistently, and, simply speaking, become successful. And stay there!

What really elevates a regular Joe or Jane to superhero status is the laser-sharp focus, perseverance, and the ability to keep on going when everyone else would have quit.
I have, for a long time, studied the lives of the most disciplined people on this planet. In this book, you are going to learn their secrets.
No matter if your goals are financial, sport, relationship, or habit-changing oriented, this book covers it all.

Today, I want to share with you the science-based insights and field-tested methods that have helped me, my friends, and my clients change their lives and become real-life go-getters.

Here are some of the things you will learn from this book:

• **What the "positive thinking trap" means,** and how exactly should you use the power of positivity to actually help yourself instead of holding yourself back?
• What truly makes us happy and how does that relate to success? Is it money? Social position? Friends, family? Health? **No. There's actually something bigger, deeper, and much more fundamental behind our happiness.** You will be surprised to find out what the factor that ultimately drives us and keeps us going is, and this discovery can greatly improve your life.
• **Why our Western perception of both happiness and success are fundamentally wrong**, and how those misperceptions can kill your chances of succeeding?
• **Why relying on willpower and motivation is a very bad idea, and what to hold on to instead?** This is as important as using only the best gasoline in a top-grade sports car. Fill its engine with a moped fuel and keep the engine oil level low, and it won't get far. Your mind is this sports car engine. I will show you where to get this quality fuel from.
• **You will learn what the common denominator of the most successful and disciplined people on this planet is** – Navy SEALS and other special forces, Shaolin monks, top performing CEOs and Athletes, they, in fact, have a lot in common. I studied their lives for a long time, and now, it's time to share this knowledge with you.
• Why your entire life can be viewed as a piece of training, and **what are the rules of this training?**
• What the XX-th century Russian Nobel-Prize winner and long-forgotten genius Japanese psychotherapist **can teach you about the importance of your emotions and utilizing them correctly in your quest to becoming a self-disciplined and a peaceful person?**
• How modern science can help you **overcome temptation and empower your will**, and why following strict and inconvenient diets or regimens can actually help you achieve your goals in the end?
• How can you win by failing and **why giving up on some of your goals can actually be a good thing?**
• How do we often become **our own biggest enemies** in achieving our goals and how to finally change it?
• How to **maintain** your success once you achieve it?

Direct Buy Link to Amazon Kindle Store:
http://tinyurl.com/IanMentalToughness
Paperback version on Createspace: http://tinyurl.com/IanMTPaperback

Accelerated Learning: The Most Effective Techniques: How to Learn Fast, Improve Memory, Save Your Time and Be Successful

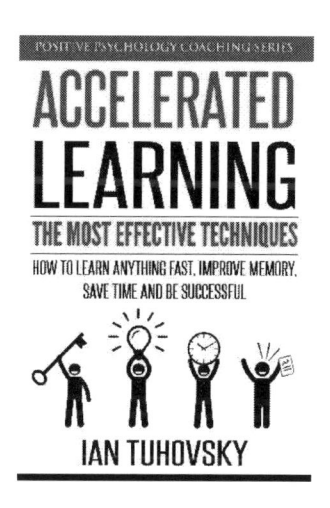

Unleash the awesome power of your brain to achieve your true potential, learn anything, and enjoy greater success than you ever thought possible.

Packed with proven methods that help you significantly improve your memory and develop simple-yet-powerful learning methods, Accelerated Learning: The Most Effective Techniques is the only brain training manual you'll ever need to master new skills, become an expert in any subject, and achieve your goals, whatever they may be.

Easy Step-by-Step Instructions Anyone Can Use Immediately

- Student preparing for crucial exams?

- Parent looking to better understand, encourage, and support your child's learning?

- Career professional hoping to develop new skills to land that dream job?

Whoever you are and whatever your reason for wanting to improve your memory, Accelerated Learning: The Most Effective Techniques will show you exactly how to do it with simple, actionable tasks that you can use to help you:

- Destroy your misconceptions that learning is difficult - leaving you free to fairly pursue your biggest passions.

- Stop procrastinating forever, eliminate distractions entirely, and supercharge your focus, no matter what the task at hand.

- Cut the amount of time it takes you to study effectively and enjoy more time away from your textbooks.

- Give yourself the best chance of success by creating your own optimal learning environment.

Everything you'll learn in this book can be implemented immediately regardless of your academic background, age, or circumstances, so no matter who you are, you can start changing your life for the better RIGHT NOW.

Take control of your future with life-changing learning skills.

Self-doubt is often one of the biggest barriers people face in realizing their full potential and enjoying true success.

In Accelerated Learning: The Most Effective Techniques, you'll not only find out how to overcome that self-doubt, but also how to thrive in any learning environment with scientifically-proven tools and techniques.

You'll also discover:
- How to use an ancient Roman method for flawless memorization of long speeches and complex information

- The secret to never forgetting anyone's name ever again.

- The easy way to learn an entirely new language, no matter how complex.

- The reason why flashcards, mind maps, and mnemonic devices haven't worked for you in the past - and how to change that.

- The simple speed-reading techniques you can use to absorb information faster.

- How to cut the amount of time it takes you to study effectively and enjoy more time away from your textbooks.

- The truth about binaural beats and whether they can help you focus.

- How to effectively cram any exam (in case of emergencies!).

And much more!

Direct Buy Link to Amazon Kindle Store:
http://getbook.at/AcceleratedLearning

Paperback version on Createspace:

http://getbook.at/AcceleratedLearningPaperback

Empath: An Empowering Book for the Highly Sensitive Person on Utilizing Your Unique Ability and Maximizing Your Human Potential

Have others ever told you to "stop being so sensitive?" Have you ever looked at other people and wondered how they manage to get through the day without noticing the suffering going on all around them?

Do you feel so emotionally delicate in comparison to your peers that you have tried to block out what is going on around you? You may have even resorted to coping mechanisms such as overeating, overworking, or smoking as a means of managing your emotions.

Maybe you have tried to "grow a thicker skin," or attempted to cover up your feelings with humor? Perhaps you have always felt different to others since childhood, but could never quite put your finger on why.

If this description resonates with you, congratulations! You may well be an Empath. **Unfortunately, an Empath who lacks insight into their own nature is likely to be miserable.**

Most of us are familiar with the concept of empathy. Aside from sociopaths, who are largely incapable of appreciating what another individual may be feeling, humans are generally able to understand what others are going through in most situations. Empaths, however, constitute the small group of people who not only understand the emotions of others, but literally feel them too.

In short, an Empath takes this common human ability of relating to other peoples' emotions to extremes.

If you have no idea why you are so readily affected by the emotions of others and the events around you, you will become psychologically unstable. You will be unsure as to where your true feelings end, and those of other people begin.

Hypersensitivity can be a burden if not properly managed, which is why it's so important that all Empaths learn to harness the special gift they have been given.

That's where this book comes in. Millions of other people around the world share your gifts and lead happy, fulfilling lives. Make no mistake – the world needs us.

It's time to learn how to put your rare gift to use, maximize your human potential, and thrive in life!

If you think you (or anyone around you) might be an Empath or the Highly Sensitive Person – this book is written for you.

What you will learn from this book:
-**What it really means to be an Empath** and the science behind the "Empath" and "the Highly Sensitive Person" classification. Find out how our brains work and why some people are way more sensitive than others.
-**What are the upsides of being an Empath** – find your strengths and thrive while making the most of your potential and providing value to this world (it NEEDS Empaths!) by making it a better place.
-**What are the usual problems that sensitive people struggle** with – overcome them by lessening the impact that other people's emotions and actions have on you, while still being truthful to your true nature, and learn how to take care of your mental health.
-**The great importance of becoming an emotionally intelligent person** – learn what EQ is and how you can actively develop it to become much more peaceful, effective, and a happy person. Discover the strategies that will help you stay balanced and be much more immune to the everyday struggles.
-**The workplace and career choices** – realize what you should be aware of and find how to make sure you don't stumble into the most common problems that sensitive people often fall prey to.
-**How to effectively handle conflicts, negative people, and toxic** relationships – since sensitive people are more much more immune to difficult relations and often become an easy target for those who tend to take advantage of others – it's time to put this to an end with this book.
-**How to deal with Empaths and Highly Sensitive People as a non-Empath** and what to focus on if you think that your kid might fall under this classification.
-**How to connect with other Empaths**, what is the importance of gender in this context, and how to stay in harmony with your environment – **you will learn all of this and more from this book!**

Direct Buy Link to Amazon Kindle Store:
http://tinyurl.com/IanEmpathKindle

Paperback version on Createspace:
http://tinyurl.com/IanEmpathPaperback

Confidence: Your Practical Training: How to Develop Healthy Self Esteem and Deep Self Confidence to Be Successful and Become True Friends with Yourself

Have you ever considered how many opportunities you have missed and how many chances you have wasted by lacking self-confidence when you need it most?

Have you ever given up on your plans, important goals, and dreams not because you just decided to focus on something else, but simply because you were too SCARED or hesitant to even start, or stick up to the plan and keep going?

Are you afraid of starting your own business or asking for a promotion? Petrified of public speaking, socializing, dating, taking up new hobbies, or going to job interviews?

Can you imagine how amazing and relieving it would feel to finally obtain all the self-esteem needed to accomplish things you've always wanted to achieve in your life?

Finally, have you ever found yourself in a situation where you simply couldn't understand **WHY you acted in a certain way**, or why you kept holding yourself back and feeling all the bad emotions, instead of just going for what's the most important to you?

Due to early social conditioning and many other influences, most people on this planet are already familiar with all these feelings.

WAY TOO FAMILIAR!

I know how it feels, too. I was in the same exact place.

And then, I found the way!
It's high time you did something about it too because, truth be told, self-confident people just have it way easier in every single aspect of life!

From becoming your own boss or succeeding in your career, through dating and socializing, to starting new hobbies, standing up for yourself or maybe finally packing your suitcase and going on this Asia trip you promised yourself decades ago... All too often, people fail in these quests as they aren't equipped with the natural and lasting self-confidence to deal with them in a proper way.

Confidence is not useful only in everyday life and casual situations. Do you really want to fulfill your wildest dreams, or do you just want to keep chatting about them with your friends, until one day you wake up as a grumpy, old, frustrated person?
Big achievements require brave and fearless actions. If you want to act bravely, you need to be confident.

Along with lots of useful, practical exercises, this book will provide you with plenty of new information that will help you understand what confidence problems really come down to. And this is the most important and the saddest part, because most people do not truly recognize the root problem, and that's why they get poor results.

Lack of self-confidence and problems with unhealthy self-esteem are usually the reason why smart, competent, and talented people never achieve a satisfying life; a life that should easily be possible for them.

In this book, you will read about:
-How, when, and why society robs us all of natural confidence and healthy self-esteem.
-What kind of social and psychological traps you need to avoid in order to feel much calmer, happier, and more confident.
-What "natural confidence" means and how it becomes natural.
-What "self-confidence" really is and what it definitely isn't (as opposed to what most people think!).
-How your mind hurts you when it really just wants to help you, and how to stop the process.
-What different kinds of fear we feel, where they come from, and how to defeat them.
-How to have a great relationship with yourself.
-How to use stress to boost your inner strength.
-Effective and ineffective ways of building healthy self-esteem.
-Why the relation between self-acceptance and stress is so crucial.
-How to stay confident in professional situations.
-How to protect your self-esteem when life brings you down, and how to deal with criticism and jealousy.
-How to use neuro-linguistic programming, imagination, visualizations, diary entries, and your five senses to re-program your subconscious and get rid of "mental viruses" and detrimental beliefs that actively destroy your natural confidence and healthy self-esteem.
Take the right action and start changing your life for the better today!

DOWNLOAD FOR FREE from Amazon Kindle Store:
https://tinyurl.com/IanConfidenceTraining
Paperback version on Createspace:
http://tinyurl.com/IanConfidencePaperbackV

Mindfulness: The Most Effective Techniques: Connect With Your Inner Self to Reach Your Goals Easily and Peacefully

Mindfulness is not about complicated and otherworldly woo-woo spiritual practices. It doesn't require you to be a part of any religion or a movement.

What mindfulness is about is living a good life (that's quite practical, right?), and this book is all about deepening your awareness, **getting to know yourself**, and developing attitudes and mental habits that will make you not only a successful and effective person in life, but a happy and wise one as well.

If you have ever wondered what the mysterious words "mindfulness" means and why would anyone bother, you have just found your (detailed) answer!

This book will provide you with actionable steps and valuable information, all in plain English, so all of your doubts will be soon gone.

In my experience, **nothing has proven as simple and yet effective and powerful as the daily practice of mindfulness.**

It has helped me become more decisive, disciplined, focused, calm, and just a happier person.

I can come as far as to say that mindfulness has transformed me into a success.

Now, it's your turn.
There's nothing to lose, and so much to win!

The payoff is nothing less than transforming your life into its true potential.

What you will learn from this book:

-What exactly does the word "mindfulness" mean, and why should it become an important word in your dictionary?

-How taking **as little as five minutes a day** to clear your mind might result in steering your life towards great success and becoming a much more fulfilled person? ...and **how the heck can you "clear your mind" exactly?**

-What are the **most interesting, effective, and not well-known mindfulness techniques for success** that I personally use to stay on the track and achieve my goals daily while feeling calm and relaxed?

-**Where to start** and how to slowly get into mindfulness to avoid unnecessary confusion?

-What are the **scientifically proven profits** of a daily mindfulness practice?

-**How to develop the so-called "Nonjudgmental Awareness"** to win with discouragement and negative thoughts, **stick to the practice** and keep becoming a more focused, calm, disciplined, and peaceful person on a daily basis?

-What are **the most common problems** experienced by practitioners of mindfulness and meditation, and how to overcome them?

-How to meditate and **just how easy** can it be?

-What are **the most common mistakes** people keep doing when trying to get into meditation and mindfulness? How to avoid them?

-**Real life tested steps** to apply mindfulness to everyday life to become happier and much more successful person?

-What is the relation between mindfulness and life success? How to use mindfulness to become much more effective in your life and achieve your goals much easier?

-**What to do in life** when just about everything seems to go wrong?

-How to become a **more patient and disciplined person**?

Stop existing and start living.
Start changing your life for the better today.

DOWNLOAD FOR FREE from Amazon Kindle Store:

myBook.to/IanMindfulnessGuide
Paperback version on Createspace:

http://tinyurl.com/IanMindfulnessGuide

About the Author

Author's blog: www.mindfulnessforsuccess.com
Author's Amazon profile: amazon.com/author/iantuhovsky
Instagram profile: https://instagram.com/mindfulnessforsuccess

Hi! I'm Ian...

. . . and I am interested in life. I am in the study of having an awesome and passionate life, which I believe is within the reach of practically everyone. I'm not a mentor or a guru. I'm just a guy who always knew there was more than we are told. I managed to turn my life around from way below my expectations to a really satisfying one, and now I want to share this fascinating journey with you so that you can do it, too.

I was born and raised somewhere in Eastern Europe, where Polar Bears eat people on the streets, we munch on snow instead of ice cream and there's only vodka instead of tap water, but since I make a living out of several different businesses, I move to a new country every couple of months. I also work as an HR consultant for various European companies.

I love self-development, traveling, recording music and providing value by helping others. I passionately read and write about social psychology, sociology, NLP, meditation, mindfulness, eastern philosophy, emotional intelligence, time management, communication skills and all of the topics related to conscious self-development and being the most awesome version of yourself.

Breathe. Relax. Feel that you're alive and smile. And never hesitate to contact me!